FRIENDLY SOCIETIES

INSTITUTE OF ACTUARIES STUDENTS' SOCIETY'S
CONSOLIDATION OF READING SERIES
Editor: C. W. KENCHINGTON, F.I.A.

FRIENDLY SOCIETIES

BY

C. H. L. BROWN, B.Sc., F.I.A.

AND

J. A. G. TAYLOR, F.I.A.

CAMBRIDGE

Published for the Institute of Actuaries Students' Society

AT THE UNIVERSITY PRESS

1944

It will be understood, of course, that the Society is
not responsible for the opinions put forward herein.

CAMBRIDGE
UNIVERSITY PRESS

University Printing House, Cambridge CB2 8BS, United Kingdom

Cambridge University Press is part of the University of Cambridge.

It furthers the University's mission by disseminating knowledge in the pursuit of
education, learning and research at the highest international levels of excellence.

www.cambridge.org
Information on this title: www.cambridge.org/9781107426108

© Cambridge University Press 1933

First published 1933
First paperback edition 2014

A catalogue record for this publication is available from the British Library

ISBN 978-1-107-42610-8 Paperback

AUTHORS' PREFACE

In the preparation of this book we have had constantly in mind the fact that whilst to the majority of students the Life Office valuation is very familiar, comparatively few have opportunities of acquiring practical experience in the work of valuing Friendly Societies, and this must be our excuse for introducing into the text matter which, although possibly obvious and commonplace, may yet lead to a more complete appreciation of the nature of the problems associated with institutions which differ so widely from Life Offices.

The volume of reading on the subject of Friendly Societies is not very extensive and, whilst we believe that the book carries out the general aim of the Consolidation of Reading series, we feel that it will best assist the student if he regards it as a preliminary to the study of more advanced reading.

We wish to take this opportunity of expressing our thanks for much advice and criticism, which have been of great value to us in the preparation of the book.

C. H. L. B.
J. A. G. T.

LONDON
October 1932

EDITOR'S PREFACE

This is the second volume of the series to be published by the Institute of Actuaries Students' Society under the title "Consolidation of Reading", and like the first it is intended to provide an introduction to the subject with which it deals.

Problems connected with the administration and valuation of Friendly Societies do not come within the daily experience of so large a number of examination students as do the problems associated with Life Office Valuation and Surplus. For this reason the present volume is to a larger extent than the former an elementary treatise on the subject with which it deals, and comparatively few references are made to existing papers. It is hoped that this connected account of the operations of Friendly Societies from the pens of two Actuaries, whose experience peculiarly fits them to be the authors of the volume, will materially assist students in making their first approach to this subject, and that they will be the better able to appreciate the more technical aspects of the problems that will confront them in their further reading.

C. W. K.

BIRMINGHAM
December 1932

TABLE OF CONTENTS

CHAPTER I
DESCRIPTION OF BENEFITS

CHAPTER II
TYPES OF SOCIETIES

CHAPTER III
LEGISLATION AFFECTING REGISTERED FRIENDLY SOCIETIES

CHAPTER IV

RULES OF REGISTERED FRIENDLY SOCIETIES

CHAPTER V

METHODS OF SUBMITTING DATA FOR INVESTI-GATION OF EXPERIENCE AND FOR VALUATION

CHAPTER VI

EXPERIENCE AND BASIS OF VALUATION

CHAPTER VII

VALUATION

CHAPTER VIII

DISTRICT FUNERAL FUNDS AND SPECIAL SICKNESS BENEFITS

CHAPTER IX

THE VALUATION REPORT

CHAPTER X

FRIENDLY SOCIETIES SINCE THE ADVENT OF NATIONAL HEALTH INSURANCE

CHAPTER I

DESCRIPTION OF BENEFITS

1. The origin of friendly societies is held by some writers to be lost in antiquity. However that may be, they certainly existed, though perhaps not under their present designation of friendly societies, centuries before 1793, when the first Act of Parliament dealing with them was passed. In most of the older societies the early activities were largely social and ritualistic, but there was always the underlying idea of mutual assistance in distress occasioned by sickness or death, and both the social and the financial sides of many friendly societies, especially of those of the affiliated orders, are still equally developed. In the early days, contributions were determined by fixing a levy sufficient to meet the current needs, only a small fund being accumulated. Regular contributions for fixed benefits were a later development, as was also the idea of investing funds as distinct from the practice of keeping the assets locked up in "the box", to which references are frequently found in the earlier rules of old-established societies.

2. The Acts of Parliament regulating the operations of friendly societies are dealt with in Chapter III, but it may be mentioned here that in 1896 an Act was passed to consolidate the law relating to them, and that their present conduct is still largely governed by that Act. The most important enactments since the Act of 1896 affecting friendly societies are the Industrial Assurance Act, 1923, the Friendly Societies Act, 1924, the Industrial Assurance and Friendly Societies Act, 1929, and the National Health Insurance Acts, although the last named, with the exception of section 72 of the 1911 Act, are concerned mainly with the transaction of State Insurance business.

3. Societies may be registered under the Friendly Societies Act, 1896, if their purposes are any of those specified in section 8 of that

Act.* In this book attention is devoted almost exclusively to those societies which in section 8 (1) are called "friendly societies".

Most friendly societies, and certainly all the larger ones, are registered, although occasionally a society of some importance is met with which is still unregistered. The privileges of registration are so great, however, that a society which wishes to compete effectively cannot afford to remain unregistered (see Chapter III, par. 6).

The more usual types of benefit are described in the following paragraphs.

SICKNESS BENEFITS

4. Sickness-benefits are cash payments, generally made weekly, to members who are unable to follow their normal occupations by reason of sickness or accident. It is very difficult to state what the term "sickness", as it is used by friendly societies, connotes, and indeed, as Watson mentions in his paper, *J.I.A.* Vol. LXII, p. 13, the rules of many societies are vague in their definition of it. In the same paper he quotes several definitions and discusses fully this subject. The amount of the payment is usually of the order of 10s. to £1 per week, but larger assurances are now becoming more common. It is important to notice that the qualification for receipt of benefit is usually inability to work or to follow the normal occupation. Almost invariably the benefit continues at the full rate for a

* Shortly, section 8 permits registration of
(1) Societies (called friendly societies) for the purpose of providing by voluntary subscriptions for
  (a) sickness and other disability benefits;
  (b) maternity and death benefits;
  (c) relief when on travel in search of employment;
  (d) endowments;
  (e) insurance against fire of tools and implements of trade.
(There are limitations on the amounts of benefit that may be assured.)
(2) Societies (called cattle insurance societies) for insurance against loss of cattle, sheep, horses, etc., by death from disease or otherwise.
(3) Societies (called benevolent societies) for any benevolent or charitable purpose.
(4) Societies (called working-men's clubs) for purposes of social intercourse, mutual helpfulness, etc.
(5) Societies (called specially authorized societies) for any purpose which the Treasury may authorize as a purpose to which the provisions of the Act...might be extended.

limited period only. This period is usually 26 weeks or 52 weeks, or occasionally longer, but shorter periods are sometimes met with, more particularly in the case of societies which have reduced their benefits as a result of a deficiency on valuation. After the period of full pay has expired the benefit is reduced to a fraction, rarely less than one-half or more than three-quarters, of full pay, and this reduction may be followed by one or more further decreases in the rate of benefit. The general practice is for the lowest rate of sick pay, which is described variously as the continuous sickness benefit, the reduced sick allowance, the long-continued sick pay, etc., to be continued as long as sickness lasts, but as some societies grant sickness benefits which terminate at the end of a short period such as 1 or 2 years, whether the member has recovered or not, it is of the utmost importance to ascertain carefully from the rules which type of benefit is provided. It will readily be appreciated that there is a vast difference between the value of a sickness benefit which may be received continuously to age 65 or 70 or throughout life, and one which is merely temporary.

5. In conjunction with the rules governing the reduction of the rate of sick pay there is usually one dealing with the "off period". Under its operation all claims not separated by a period at least equal to the off period are linked up, and treated as one continuous claim for the purpose of determining both the rate of benefit payable and when it shall be reduced. The rule applies both to the reduction from full pay to reduced pay and to further reductions, although the length of the off period is not necessarily the same in each case. The most usual off period is 52 weeks, but its duration varies widely, periods as short as 13 weeks or as long as 4 or 5 years being occasionally found. The length of the off period exercises an important influence over the society's sickness experience. The off period prevents a member from avoiding a reduction in the rate of benefit, as by its operation he is precluded from drawing full pay for a period practically equal to the whole of the full-pay period, declaring off the funds for a short time only, and then again commencing shortly afterwards a fresh full period of benefit at the maximum rate. It may here be mentioned that the standard off

period adopted in the analysis of the Manchester Unity 1893–97 Experience was 52 weeks. Many societies insist on a medical certificate of recovery being produced before the member is allowed to resume work, and a medical certificate is always required periodically whilst sickness benefit is being claimed.

6. Societies which do not grant a continuous benefit often allow the member to resume benefit at the full rate when he has exhausted the prescribed periods of reduced pay, after the expiration of a definite period, usually one or more years. This is a type of benefit which requires special treatment in valuation.

7. Numerous limitations of benefit have been devised by societies to safeguard their funds. Among them may be mentioned the limitation of the total amount of sick pay which may be received throughout the whole duration of membership. This is effected either by restricting the total number of weeks of sick pay, or the number of weeks at the full or half-rate, or by placing a limit upon the total amount of sickness benefit receivable. When the member has received the total amount of benefit payable, he is usually allowed to pay a reduced contribution for the death benefit only, for, if no reduction were made, the member, unless seriously ill, would allow his membership to lapse. A few societies pay a reduced benefit, or more rarely no benefit at all, in cases of industrial accident or disease in respect of which the member is entitled to claim compensation under the Workmen's Compensation Acts.

Usually a member is required to have been in the society for 6 or 12 months before being entitled to sick pay, and this period is known as the "waiting period". In some cases half-benefit is allowed during the second half of the waiting period.

8. The tables of benefit adopted in recent years have in increasing numbers provided for sickness benefits and contributions ceasing at the definite age of either 65 or 70 years, whereas before the National Insurance Act, 1911, was passed they usually provided for benefits and contributions payable throughout life. Termination at age 70 is the more usual, although the necessity for terminating sickness benefits at age 65 is becoming more generally recognized now that pension benefits are claimable under the State scheme at

that age. There still persists a reluctance on the part of the management of some friendly societies to adopt this limitation, but there is no doubt in the minds of those best qualified to judge, that the right to claim sickness benefit contemporaneously with the receipt of a pension will lead to so considerable an increase in the expenditure on sickness benefits that societies will eventually be compelled to cease granting sickness benefits beyond the age of 65. Attention was drawn earlier in this chapter to the fact that the qualification for sickness benefit is incapacity for work by reason of sickness, and it is manifestly difficult to determine whether a member who is not normally employed is qualified to receive sick pay. There is, also, the consideration that a man who is partially provided for by way of pension and who is not dependent solely on his employment will be more inclined to claim sickness benefit than one who is dependent almost entirely on his employment. In the former case the receipt of sick pay probably forms an increase in his income, whilst in the latter the amount of sick pay is generally less than the man's normal earnings.

Death Benefits

9. Death benefits are frequently included with sickness, or sickness and annuity benefits, under one contract. In the case of the large friendly societies this is almost invariably so, and the practice is to be commended, for, as will be explained in a later chapter, light mortality tends as a rule to increase the cost of sickness benefits, and the inclusion of death benefits in the same fund partly counterbalances this effect. Where separate funds are maintained for the different types of benefit it is not unusual to find that, whilst the sickness fund is barely solvent, the death fund possesses a surplus. The amount of the member's death benefit is frequently as many pounds as there are shillings in the amount of full weekly sick pay for which he is insured, whilst the wife's death benefit, payable only if she pre-deceases her husband, is often one-half the member's benefit. The practice in regard to the insurance of second wives varies considerably. In some societies a separate assurance, at an equitable rate of contribution, has to be entered upon by the member on re-marriage, whilst in others he merely pays a nominal

registration fee. In exceptional cases no fee or contribution is charged.

10. A practice frequently followed by societies is to allow the widow of a deceased member to continue to be assured with the society for the same amount as that for which she was assured during her husband's lifetime, for a small quarterly contribution. The contribution is usually inadequate to provide the benefit, but friendly societies are inclined to look at smaller matters of this description rather from the standpoint of sentiment than of sound finance.

11. One important variation of the death benefit often met with is the provision for the payment of one-half of the death benefit at the first death whether it be of the husband or of the wife, the other half being an absolute assurance on the death of the member. This condition is usually contained in a rule which states that one-half of the death benefit may be drawn by the member at the death of his wife.

12. In the case of Widows' and Orphans' Funds, which are commonly associated with branches of the larger friendly societies, the death benefit, which is only payable as a rule provided the member leaves a widow or orphans, often takes the form of an increasing assurance, the benefit increasing regularly year by year or after periods of membership of 5, 7 or 10 years until the maximum amount is reached. An additional amount may be payable on the death of a member in respect of each of his children under the age of 14 or 16. Occasionally a small benefit is payable to a member on the death of a child under a specified age, often without the child's being registered in the books of the fund. In some societies a benefit smaller than the amount of the widow's benefit is payable to a nominee when the member does not leave a widow or orphans.

The death benefit payable to a widow out of such funds sometimes takes the form of a term-certain annuity, or, less frequently, a life annuity.

13. Other minor benefits payable at death are those provided by Jewish societies. They include the shiva, or confined mourning benefit, which is a variable cash sum dependent upon the performance of specific rites, payable to the member on the death of a near relative, and a small addition to the member's death benefit, intended to cover the cost of a tombstone.

ANNUITY BENEFITS

14. Annuity benefits, except in the case of the older county and local societies, have only comparatively recently received much attention from friendly societies, but consequent upon the more general adoption of sickness benefits ceasing at age 65 or 70 the provision of this form of benefit is becoming more common. When an annuity is included with sickness and death benefits for one indivisible contribution, no contributions are returned if death occurs before the pension age is reached, but where separate contributions are payable two tables are sometimes used, the one providing for the return of the contributions paid, either with or without interest, but usually without interest, and the other for no return of contributions.

ENDOWMENT BENEFITS

15. Except in the case of collecting societies, pure endowments, both with and without return of premiums, and endowment assurances, though frequently provided for in the rules, are not taken up in large numbers.

MATERNITY BENEFITS

16. The largest centralized society, the Hearts of Oak Benefit Society, provides a maternity benefit as part of the normal benefits of male members. Apart from this example, however, maternity benefits are comparatively rare, although female members of some of the smaller societies and of a branch here and there of the affiliated orders are entitled to this benefit. The benefit, as in the case of the National Insurance Scheme, takes the form of a lump sum payment which varies from about 10s. to £2.

DISTRESS AND OTHER BENEFITS

17. Distress benefits are usually discretionary cash payments made out of a separate fund supported by a small contribution and often by transfers from surplus. They are, however, sometimes paid out of the benefit funds. The objects for which payments may be made are governed by the rules and often include grants to members or their widows and orphans; subscriptions to hospitals, infirmaries, charitable or provident institutions; travelling relief to members when in search of work, and the payment of members' contributions.

Subsidiary benefits which friendly societies may, and occasionally do, grant are the insurance of tools against fire up to a maximum of £15, and convalescent-home treatment.

Guarantee of Officials

18. Societies are entitled to establish a fund or a separate society for the purpose of guaranteeing the performance of their duties by officers or servants of the society. This power is, however, rarely exercised except by the larger societies.

Unemployment Benefits

19. Unemployment benefits are granted for the most part by the type of society known as Clerks', or Warehousemen's and Clerks' Associations and are generally associated with a sickness benefit which is, however, usually subject to the condition that it is not payable unless salary be stopped. The total amount which may be drawn under both headings within certain periods of membership is generally limited to a fixed sum.

Medical Benefit

20. A medical benefit was formerly provided by the majority of friendly societies, but the introduction of the National Health Scheme rendered it unnecessary for them to continue to arrange for this benefit except for the small minority of members who were not State-insured. The contribution charged was usually the amount paid to the doctor, and although the cost of the benefit has risen in recent years the contribution has not always been correspondingly increased. In such cases the society's funds are liable for the deficit.

CHAPTER II

TYPES OF SOCIETIES

THE AFFILIATED ORDERS

1. Both numerically and financially the affiliated orders constitute the largest group of the various types of friendly societies. Apart from variations in points of detail these orders are similarly constituted. The lodge (or court or tent) is the unit, lodges in the same locality are aggregated into districts and above the district is the central governing body of the order.

2. The lodges, each of which is separately registered under the Friendly Societies Act, are independent units governed by their own elected officers. These usually consist of a chairman and vice-chairman (described in the different orders by various but always picturesque names) and a committee of management, all of whom are elected to office for a fixed term, usually one year. The secretary and treasurer are permanent officials elected to continue in office during the pleasure of the lodge. The lodge elects representatives to the district meeting, the number of delegates depending upon numerical strength, and the district officers are elected at the district meeting. The district meeting elects representatives to the annual conference of the order, and it is at this annual conference that the governing body of the order is elected.

3. The member's contract is made with the lodge, which receives the contributions and pays out the benefits. The death benefits, payable on the death of a member and of a member's wife, are frequently re-assured with a district fund, which may be supported either by a system of levies under which only sufficient money is raised to meet current claims or by fixed contributions involving the accumulation of a reserve fund. These district funds constitute an important bond of union between the various lodges of the district. Lodges are valued as separate units, and, subject to the formal approval of the central executive body, the members have the right to allocate for any purpose in conformity with the general rules of the order, the surplus available for appropriation. The lodge has the right to secede from the order, but withdrawal is a course of action not to be undertaken lightly owing to the onerous penalties attaching thereto. It has also the right to dissolve provided it obtains the consent of the central executive body of the order. In actual practice, however, it is doubtful whether such consent would be given, and the only practical course would be for the lodge to exercise its right to secede and then voluntarily dissolve.

4. Although, as already stated, the lodges as constituted are self-governing units, the tendency has of late years been to place more power in the hands of both the district and the central body of the order. In the Manchester Unity, for instance, although the lodge appoints its own auditor, the district must appoint a "panel" auditor (the panel is recruited from members of the district whose qualifications are considered satisfactory to the district) to act with the lodge auditor, and the panel auditor must submit a report to the District Management Committee. The district also has the power to require a lodge to invest any money on hand or to realize any investment and re-invest the money to better advantage. The society has for many years possessed a central Unity Reserve Fund from which assistance is afforded to lodges in deficiency. Some few years ago the objects of the fund were considerably extended, and not only were all lodges in deficiency on valuation granted a credit sufficient to reduce the deficiency to an amount equal to 5 per cent. of the liabilities but, in addition, all lodges which had at any time suffered a reduction of benefits or an increase of contributions, were permitted to revert to the benefits and contributions originally in force. The fund, which is now supported almost entirely by definite charges on surplus, is administered by the central body, and, before becoming entitled to a grant from the fund, deficiency lodges are required by rule to comply with certain conditions mainly of an administrative character. The scheme was launched at a most opportune time and its financial success has been assured as a result of the remarkable surpluses earned by the wealthier lodges during the period of light sickness claims and high interest yields which followed its adoption.

CENTRALIZED SOCIETIES

5. Next in financial and numerical importance to the affiliated orders are the centralized societies. As the name implies, this type of society differs from that already described in that the administration is entirely in the hands of the central body, or committee of management, the members of which are elected at the annual delegate meeting. For the purpose of representation at this meeting the society is divided into areas, the number of delegates from each area depending upon its numerical strength. These societies usually employ local agents, although until a few years ago the largest of them, the Hearts of Oak Benefit Society, required its members to send all contributions by post direct to Head Office. Of recent years this society too has adopted the agency system, and the contributions are now collected and forwarded to Head Office by agents, although the payment of benefits is still made by post from Head Office. The effective supervision of sick members is more difficult for a centralized society, which has members spread over the whole country, than for a lodge which is a small unit comprising members who normally reside within a few miles at most of the lodge room. A small lodge in which each member is personally interested, and known individually to his fellow-members, must have some advantages from the point of view of minimizing unjustifiable claims. On the other hand centralization results in increased efficiency in other directions, and the balance of advantage is not necessarily with the local society or lodge.

SEMI-CENTRALIZED SOCIETIES

6. The semi-centralized societies are often said to possess the evils of both of the two constitutions already described without the advantages of either. These societies are of the "order" type, inasmuch as they consist of the aggregation of small units or lodges although without the intervening district. These units, the members of which elect their own officers, exist, however, merely for the purpose of collecting contributions and paying out benefits and for social intercourse. They are in no way self-governing, are not separately registered, and are not treated as separate units for valuation purposes. One of the difficulties under which this type of society labours is that the sickness benefit is administered by local units which, unlike the self-governing lodges in the affiliated orders, are not themselves called upon to bear the ultimate responsibility, and this not infrequently results in a comparatively unfavourable sickness experience. Another rather unfavourable feature of this type of society, which is also inherent in the system, is the somewhat heavy cost of administration per head of the membership.

7. Under this heading may be included the old-established county societies which have a number of branches with local secretaries throughout the county. Their membership is, however, drawn from a more limited field and the two inherent disadvantages attaching to the semi-centralized society previously mentioned are thereby reduced to a minimum. One feature peculiar to many of these societies is that separate contributions are paid for each type of benefit and separate and distinct funds, requiring separate valuation, are maintained. The tendency now is for these separate funds to be amalgamated wherever possible. It is sometimes found that the progressive improvement in the vitality of the members has placed the sickness fund in deficiency and the funeral fund in substantial surplus. As the majority of the members contribute to both funds, amalgamation is the obvious remedy.

LOCAL SOCIETIES

8. The local societies, although many in number, are not correspondingly strong numerically. Some are still unregistered, although the introduction of the National Health Insurance Scheme in 1911 caused many then unregistered to seek registration, whilst a considerable number amalgamated with other societies or became registered branches of the affiliated orders. Great variations in the conditions governing the receipt of sickness benefit, and in the benefit itself, are met with in the rules of these societies, and whilst many are financially sound others are in serious deficiency—usually as a result of the inadequacy of the contributions.

RAILWAY SOCIETIES

9. Membership of these societies is usually confined to wages-grade employees in the service of the railway companies, although in some societies a separate section is maintained for "out-members"—that is, members who have left the service of the company. Most of these societies are now officially recognized by the companies, although this official recognition may only carry with it the privilege of having the contributions deducted from wages. In some cases, however, definite financial assistance is afforded. These societies are governed by the usual permanent officials and a committee of management, the latter elected at the annual meeting of delegates, for the purpose of representation at which the membership is divided into areas. The company is, as a rule, entitled to be represented on the committee of management of any society to which it grants financial assistance.

COLLECTING FRIENDLY SOCIETIES

10. All collecting friendly societies must be registered under the Friendly Societies Act, 1896. The business transacted by these societies consists mainly of industrial whole life assurances, although some of the more important societies also issue pure endowment and endowment assurance contracts and in addition transact a considerable amount of ordinary business. The premiums are collected by agents. It is of interest to note that contracts assuring combined sickness and funeral benefits may come within the definition of industrial assurance business, although only one composite contribution may be payable. If the provisions of section 1 (2) of the Industrial Assurance Act, 1923, apply, the free policy and surrender value rights conferred by this Act attach to the funeral benefit portion of the contract. The larger collecting societies operate throughout the whole country in the same way as the industrial assurance companies, but many of the smaller societies confine their operations to a limited area. The government of these societies is very similar in principle to that already described in the case of the centralized societies. The members of the committee of management may be elected for a term of one or more years but very rarely fail to secure re-election at the expiration of the term. In many of these societies the right is given to the agent to nominate his successor, who must, however, be approved by the committee of management. This right of nomination is of considerable financial value and the practice of selling books to nominees constitutes the "book interest"

SPECIALLY AUTHORIZED SOCIETIES

11. The great majority of the specially authorized societies which have secured registration under the 1896 Act have for their object the provision of benefits which cannot be subjected to actuarial valuation and consequently need not be considered here. Of the remainder, membership of which is usually confined to members of a particular trade or profession, the type of benefit most frequently met with is benefit during unemployment or absence from work on account of sickness, the former not being specifically mentioned in section 8 (1) of the Act. Usually the benefit is payable only when salary is stopped, although in rare instances full or half-benefit is payable in sickness whilst the member is still in receipt of salary. It is not unusual for these societies to limit the total amount of sickness and unemployment benefit receivable, a safeguard to which may perhaps be attributed in some measure their sound financial position. Some of these societies have received financial assistance in the form of donations from employers in the trade.

DEPOSIT, HOLLOWAY AND DIVIDING SOCIETIES

12. The special feature of these societies is that reserves calculated on an actuarial basis are not accumulated. At the end of each year (or other fixed period) the excess of the income over expenditure, after providing for transfers to special reserve funds, interest on members' deposit accounts, etc., is divided amongst the members and, according to the type of society, credited to their individual accounts or distributed in cash.

13. In the case of deposit societies the contributions are either paid wholly into a common fund, or, as is the case with the largest of these societies (a society which alone accounts for more than

60 per cent. of the total membership of deposit societies), the contribution is divided, one part being paid into the common fund and the other direct into the member's individual account. In this event, when the member falls sick, a proportion of his sickness benefit is payable from his own account, the remainder being drawn from the common fund, and when his own deposit account is exhausted, his right to draw sick pay from the common fund ceases, except that for a limited period he is entitled to "grace pay". As a member is not allowed to pay additional sums into his deposit account whilst he is sick, he may, if he is unfortunate enough to encounter an extended illness before he has been able to build up a substantial deposit, soon find himself unable to draw sickness benefit. The deposit accounts are built up by the proportion, if any, of the contributions credited to the account, the annual dividend, interest on the amount of the deposit and other lump sums, not exceeding a fixed amount per annum ($£30$ in the case of one society), which the member may be able to deposit. On the attainment of a fixed age or on previous death the whole of the sum in the deposit account may be withdrawn, whilst on withdrawal from the society a portion of the sum is retained by the society, the remainder being paid to the member. There are many variations in the method of working these societies.

14. The distinctive feature of the Holloway societies is that the contribution increases with the age of the member during the greater part of the period of his membership, and is fixed at an amount which is normally more than sufficient to cover the current cost of sickness claims. The whole of the sickness benefit is payable from the society's benefit fund. As in the case of deposit societies, on the attainment of the age at which the sickness benefits cease or on previous death, or on withdrawal from the society, the whole or a portion of the amount in the deposit account may be withdrawn.

15. The dividing societies, instead of retaining the share of "profit" and crediting it, as in the case of deposit and Holloway societies, to the member's deposit account, pay it in cash to the members as a dividend. The dangers of the method of working employed by dividing societies are too well known to need elaboration.

CHAPTER III

LEGISLATION AFFECTING REGISTERED FRIENDLY SOCIETIES

1. The object of this chapter is to furnish the student with an outline of the Acts of Parliament governing the operations of friendly societies, such as will enable him to read the various Acts with discrimination, and to grasp the significance of those sections which have an actuarial aspect. The more important features of these Acts will be briefly referred to and commented upon, but it must be particularly emphasized that the actual text of those sections which have an actuarial bearing should be carefully read and studied.

2. The first Act of Parliament dealing with friendly societies was passed in 1793 and is entitled "An Act for the Encouragement and Relief of Friendly Societies". The title indicates the benevolent attitude which the government adopted towards these organizations, which are referred to in the Act as "Societies of good fellowship", and the same attitude has persisted throughout the numerous amending and consolidating Acts since passed. The principal requirements of the Act of 1793 were that the rules were to be exhibited to the Justices in Quarter Sessions, who might either annul or confirm them, and were to be signed by the Clerk of the Peace and deposited with him. A concession was made to friendly societies by exempting officers' bonds from the payment of stamp duty.

3. An important principle was introduced by the Act of 1819 which prescribed that the Justices were not to confirm tables unless they had been approved by two 'persons "known to be professional actuaries or persons skilled in calculation".

4. In 1829 it was found necessary to pass a consolidating and amending Act. Under this Act all rules had to be submitted to the barrister-at-law appointed to certify the rules of savings banks, and tables were not to be approved unless they might be adopted with safety. Societies enrolled prior to 1828 were granted the privilege of depositing funds at the Bank of England bearing interest at the rate of 3*d*. per cent. per diem, i.e. £4. 11*s*. 3*d*. per cent. per annum—in those days a valuable concession. Under this Act societies were exempted from the payment of stamp duty and were for the first time compelled to submit schedules giving particulars of their experience.

5. In 1846 an Act was passed defining the objects of a friendly society, and in 1850 a further Act was passed which required societies to submit quinquennial returns to the Registrar in order that tables might be constructed from them. Between 1850 and 1875 the hitherto almost continuous flow of legislation diminished, but in 1875 an important Act was passed which consolidated the previous legislation and established several new principles. A central office was created, two of the duties of which were to circulate information and to cause tables to be constructed. Registered societies granting annuities were to have their tables certified by an actuary appointed by the Treasury and provision was made for the first time for an actuarial valuation. Societies were compelled to submit their accounts to an annual audit and to furnish annual returns to the Registrar.

The Friendly Societies Act, 1896

6. The principal Act governing the operations of friendly societies is the consolidating Act of 1896, which incorporates most of the provisions of the Act of 1875, practically the whole of which was repealed.

The early sections of the Act deal with the Registry Office and its constitution, and it is of interest to observe the provision that the central office shall "cause to be constructed and published tables for the payment of sums of money on death, in sickness, or old age, etc.".

7. The student should note that sections 8 (1) and 41, which specified the maximum amount of benefit that could be granted by a registered friendly society, have since been amended by the 1908 Act, which enacts that no person is entitled to receive an annuity exceeding £52 per annum or a gross sum at death exceeding £300 (exclusive of any bonus added) from any one or more registered friendly societies.

A society granting annuities is required to have its annuity tables certified by an actuary (section 16), but, in contrast with the Act of 1819, tables insuring other benefits do not need certification. The Registrar indeed has no power to refuse to register an amendment of rules on the ground that its effect would be to grant benefits wholly unwarranted by the contribution payable or the financial condition of the society; but he does, in fact, exercise considerable influence in the guidance of societies in these matters. A note should be taken of section 17 (2), which states that a society having a fund under the control of a central body, to which every branch is bound to contribute, may be registered as a single society.

8. The consequences of registration are contained in sections 23–31 and are important. Section 23 provides that a subscription shall not be recoverable at law, and it is relevant here to mention that membership of a friendly society does not imply that an unalterable contract has been established between the member and the society unless the rules specially provide for it. In fact scales of benefit can be and are increased or reduced by the simple expedient of an amendment of rule.

9. The annual audit is dealt with in section 26. The audit may be performed by two or more persons appointed as the rules provide, and these persons are usually members of the society. It is a weakness of this section of the Act that the auditors may be persons with no qualification whatever for undertaking the work. There is at least one authenticated case in which the auditor certified the correctness of the accounts by endorsing them as follows: "Audited and found correct. John Brown. X (his mark)". Whether the form of certificate was due to a temporary disability or to a more obvious cause is not known. In order to comply with section 27, a registered friendly society must submit annual returns, and it may be mentioned that one of the conditions under which public valuers

hold their appointments is that they should obtain copies of the annual returns for at least the five years preceding the date of the valuation.

10. Once at least in every five years a registered society or branch is required either to arrange for a valuation to be made and to send to the Registrar a report together with an abstract of the valuation, or to send to the Registrar returns of the benefits assured, etc., in which case the Registrar will arrange for the valuation to be carried out. The latter course is believed to be unusual, and a comparison of sections 339 and 342 of the *Guide Book** will, perhaps, suggest the reason. The official form used in connection with the valuation of a friendly society is known as form F 40 (or C 28 in the case of a collecting friendly society). The Treasury are empowered to appoint public auditors and public valuers and to determine their maximum rates of remuneration, but societies may if they please place their valuations and audits in the hands of persons of their own choosing. It is an anomaly that so important a matter as valuation can thus be entrusted to a person without actuarial qualifications. Numerous special societies are entitled to exemption from valuation and a comprehensive list is given in the *Guide Book*.

11. The advantages of registration are set out *in extenso* in section 24 of the *Guide Book*. Many of them may not appear at first sight to be of very great value but in actual practice they are. It should be remembered that many friendly societies are managed by persons who are not well qualified to cope with the intricacies of the law, and as many of the privileges enjoyed by friendly societies make administration much easier, they are (quite apart from their financial significance) really important. One privilege of very great financial value is the right of a registered society to exemption from the payment of income tax, and this privilege alone makes it almost essential for a friendly society to become registered, in order that, in these days of high rates of tax, it may be able to compete with other registered societies. This privilege is not conferred by the

* *The Guide Book of the Registry of Friendly Societies and the Office of the Industrial Assurance Commissioner* (H.M. Stationery Office, 2s.). Every student should possess his own copy of this useful book of reference.

Friendly Societies Act, however, but by the Income Tax Acts (see Income Tax Act, 1918, section 39).

12. The powers of investment are wide, but all the modes of investment which it is desired to employ should be mentioned in the rules. Section 50 is an important one as it provides that, in the case of the death of one of the trustees in whom the property of the society is vested, the property shall vest without conveyance or assignment in the remaining trustees and the succeeding trustee, though in the case of government stocks a transfer is necessary. The privilege of investment with the National Debt Commissioners conferred in the very early days a considerable benefit on friendly societies. This advantage has since been nullified by the reduction in the rate of interest offered by the Commissioners and by the rise in the market rate of interest, although it is conceivable that in the future it may become of value again.

13. Section 62 has been amended by the Friendly Societies Act, 1924, and it is now enacted that:

A society or branch, whether registered or unregistered, shall not insure or pay on the death of a child under the ages hereinafter specified any sum of money which exceeds or which, when added to any amount payable on the death of that child by any other society or branch or by any trade union or industrial assurance company exceeds, the amounts hereinafter specified; that is to say:

(*a*) In the case of a child under three years of age, six pounds;

(*b*) In the case of a child under six years of age, ten pounds;

(*c*) In the case of a child under ten years of age, fifteen pounds.

It should be noted that any society, whether registered or unregistered, to which there is presented a certificate of the death of a child which does not purport to be the first (all certificates of the same death have to be numbered in consecutive order—see section 64 (3)) is bound to enquire whether any and what sums have been paid on the same death by any other society and to modify its own payment accordingly (section 66).

14. The remainder of the Act deals with disputes, amalgamation and conversion of societies, inspection, dissolution, offences and legal proceedings and other matters of mainly legal interest. The provisions of the Act in regard to the dissolution of societies are contained in sections 78–80, and these require careful study. A registered society or branch may be dissolved either of its own volition in accordance with sections 78 and 79 or by an award of the Chief Registrar in accordance with section 80. In the latter case an award of dissolution follows an investigation of the affairs of the society by the Chief Registrar upon the application of a proportion of the members (the required proportions are mentioned in sub-section (1)). The conditions upon which such an application may be made are contained in sub-section (2), from which it is clear that there must be adequate grounds for requesting the Registrar to make such an investigation. The Registrar, moreover, has the power to suspend his award for such a period as he may deem necessary to enable the society to adopt such measures as will in his judgment prevent the necessity of the award of dissolution being made. It should be noted that every award under this section, whether for dissolution or distribution of funds, is final and conclusive.

In the case of voluntary dissolution, it is very important to note section 78 (1) (c), which requires "the consent of five-sixths in value of the members (including honorary members, if any), testified by their signatures to the instrument of dissolution, and also the written consent of every person receiving or entitled to receive any relief, annuity, or other benefit from the funds of the society or branch, unless the claim of that person is first duly satisfied, or adequate provision made for satisfying that claim" before the society may dissolve. The method to be adopted in ascertaining the value of members is given in section 70 (6). In passing, it may be mentioned that similar conditions apply in the case of an amalgamation or a transfer of engagements, except that in these cases the Registrar may, under certain conditions, order that any of the assents, consents, and conditions required by the Act may be dispensed with (section 70). The procedure on voluntary dissolution is to register, in the same manner as an amendment of rules, an instrument of dissolution, and the particulars required to be set forth in the instrument are contained in section 79 (1). The requirements mentioned above in regard to persons receiving benefits are regarded as being of primary importance, for section 79 (4) directs that the instrument shall not contain any provision for a division or appropriation of the funds otherwise than for the purpose of carrying into effect the objects of the society unless those claims have first been duly satisfied.

The National Insurance Acts

15. The most important provision of these Acts in their relation to friendly societies is section 72 of the Act of 1911. Under this section every registered friendly society which provided benefits similar to any of those conferred by the National Insurance Act, 1911, was obliged to submit a scheme for continuing, abolishing, or altering such benefits as respects those of its members who became insured persons and for adjusting their contributions correspondingly. The section laid down the principle that the scheme was not to affect prejudicially the solvency of the society. In those cases in which a large proportion of the membership elected to reduce their benefits the financial position of the society was improved considerably as a result of the release of the reserves required to provide sickness benefits until age 70 was reached. The majority of members of friendly societies, however, elected to continue their full benefits from their societies and to receive the State benefits in addition. The maximum reduction in the member's contribution allowable under the scheme was 17s. 4d. per annum, but, as in many instances the society previously provided medical aid at a cost of 4s. 4d. per annum or thereabouts, the actual amount of the reduction in the contribution to the society's benefit fund for which provision had to be made was in many cases about 13s. per annum only, and on a reasonable basis of valuation the value of the benefits given up exceeded the value of the reduction of contributions except at the younger ages.

Industrial Assurance Act, 1923

16. This Act, which repealed the Collecting Societies and Industrial Assurance Companies Act, 1896, and which, in parts, is difficult to construe, applies to collecting friendly societies as well as to industrial assurance companies. Registered friendly societies which do not collect premiums at a greater distance than 10 miles from the registered office by means of collectors may in accordance with section 10 be exempted from the provisions of the Act. The general purpose of the Act is to afford greater protection to the policy-owner, and most of its provisions are directed to this end. Particularly important sections are 23, 24, 25 and 32, which deal with the forfeiture of policies and the right to free paid-up policies or, in certain circumstances, to surrender values. The following observations may be of assistance to the student in his first reading of this Act.

17. The opening words of the Act, "Industrial assurance business shall not be carried on except by a registered friendly society or an industrial assurance company", should be noted. Industrial assurance business was formerly carried on by societies which were unregistered and not subject to any form of surveillance. After the passing of the Act these societies had either to seek registration and, as a consequence, deposit £20,000 unless exempted conditionally from so doing by the Industrial Assurance Commissioner, or to wind up or to transfer their engagements to a registered friendly society or an assurance company.

18. The main definition of industrial assurance business is that it is the effecting of assurances upon human life, premiums in respect of which are payable at intervals of less than two months, and are received by means of collectors. There are various exclusions from this definition, for particulars of which reference should be made to section 1 of the 1923 Act.

19. The maximum amounts which may be insured or paid by industrial assurance companies and collecting societies on the death of children were increased to the limits already detailed in paragraph 13 above, but the increased limits did not apply to friendly societies as distinct from collecting societies. The matter was rectified by a short Act passed in 1924.

20. Every collecting society is required to keep separate accounts and to form a separate fund for its industrial assurance business, but the investments of this fund need not be kept separate from the investments of the other funds. Separate valuations are required of the industrial assurance business, and all collecting societies were required to have the first valuation made under the Act as at a date not later than 31st December, 1925. In numerous cases where separate funds had not been kept a division of the funds was made in conjunction with the first valuation.

21. The rules of the society must contain the tables under which the industrial policies are issued and no other policies are allowed to be issued. A number of sections of the Act have to be incorporated in the rules.

22. The accounts of a collecting society must be audited by a public auditor, whereas other friendly societies can still have their accounts audited either by a public auditor or by two persons appointed in accordance with the rules of the society. The Commissioner may reject any return which is incorrect or incomplete.

23. The powers of the Commissioner in regard to an inspection of a collecting society are contained in section 17 and are very wide.

24. Section 18, which contains the provisions as to valuations, is very important. Valuations of a collecting society must be made by an actuary, as defined in the section, whereas valuations of a friendly society may be made by anyone who chooses to style himself a valuer. The basis of valuation is directed to be such as to place a proper value upon the liabilities, regard being had to the rate of interest earned, the mortality experience and the expenses of management (including commission), although no actual basis of valuation is laid down. The basis upon which minimum free paid-up policies and surrender values must be calculated is however prescribed in the Fourth Schedule. In the case of other friendly societies no such statutory conditions as to the valuation basis apply, and there is thus a fundamental distinction between the two types of societies. The Commissioner is empowered, moreover, to reject a valuation which does not comply with the provisions of this section and to direct the society to make such alterations as may be necessary to comply therewith. He may also ask for such further particulars as are mentioned in the Second Schedule to the Act and for such explanations in connection with the valuation as he may

require in order to satisfy himself that it complies with the provisions of the section. It should be noted also that the Commissioner
has power in a case where the valuation discloses a deficiency to
award that the society be dissolved if he is satisfied after investigation that its position is such as to warrant that treatment. It will
be appreciated therefore that a grave responsibility rests upon
the actuary who makes the valuation.

25. As has already been mentioned, the general purpose of the Act
is to protect the policy-owner, and sections 20–31, dealing with the
rights of owners of policies, demand careful attention, especially
sections 24 and 25. Before an industrial policy can be lapsed, notice
must be served stating the amount of premiums due and requiring
payment thereof within 28 days, and it is of interest to note that in
the case of a collecting society this procedure applies to all contracts
of assurance, whether industrial or not. Where a notice of forfeiture
has been served the owner of a policy for a term of less than 25 years
on which three years' premiums have been paid, or of a policy for
the whole term of life or for a term of more than 25 years on which
five years' premiums have been paid (subject, however, to the
condition that in the case of a whole life policy or an endowment
for a term of 50 years or upwards the person whose life is assured
has attained the age of 15), is entitled within one year to claim a free
paid-up policy—or in the particular circumstances defined in
section 24 (1) (ii) a surrender value—calculated in accordance with
the provisions of the Act.

26. The rights of an owner of a policy who agrees to accept a new
policy in substitution therefor are set forth in section 25, and it is
important to notice that it is incumbent upon the society to see that
the policy-holder secures his rights without the necessity of applying
for them. The section provides that the owner is entitled to the
surrender value of the old policy or to a free paid-up policy of
equivalent value, unless a new policy is issued with such an addition
to the normal amount assured as would result (when the policy is
valued in accordance with the rules of the Fourth Schedule to the
Act) in its having a value equal to or exceeding the surrender value
of the old policy. In the latter event a statement of account has to

be rendered. The rules of the Fourth Schedule imply that a policy can have a value after it has been in force for two years (except in the case of entrants under 10 years, when the term may be longer), and section 29 (2) defines the surrender value as 75 per cent. of the value of the policy.

27. An owner of a forfeited policy is entitled to a surrender value in accordance with section 24 if he submits satisfactory proof of his intention to make his permanent residence outside Great Britain, the Isle of Man and the Channel Islands, or if the person whose life is assured has disappeared and his existence is in doubt. When a doubt arises as to the continued existence of the life assured the Commissioner is empowered under section 32 (2) to award that a surrender value shall be paid in complete discharge of all claims. It will be noticed that the main claim under the 1923 Act is for a free paid-up policy, whereas under the 1929 Act referred to in later paragraphs either a free paid-up policy or a surrender value may be claimed by the owner of the policy at his option.

A statutory surrender value must also be paid under the provisions of section 5 in respect of an illegal policy issued before the Act came into operation, whilst in the case of an illegal policy issued subsequently, but not as a result of any false representation on the part of the proposer, the premiums paid must be returned in full.

28. The particulars required in connection with the valuations of collecting societies are more detailed than those for other friendly societies. The additional particulars are contained in the Second Schedule, but students should examine carefully the official form of abstract of valuation required for collecting societies (form C 28). The Fourth Schedule deals with the method of valuing policies for the purpose of ascertaining free paid-up policies and surrender values, and of course requires detailed study.

INDUSTRIAL ASSURANCE AND FRIENDLY SOCIETIES ACT, 1929

29. The purpose of this Act is clearly stated in the preamble. The necessity for the Act arose out of a ruling in a Court of Summary Jurisdiction that a society had committed an offence by paying on the death of a child under the age of 10 more than the

full statutory benefit, although the payment represented the return of premiums under an endowment policy. The opportunity was taken in drafting the 1929 Act to validate the issue of "life of another" endowment assurance policies within the prescribed degrees of relationship, provided that the sum assured was not in excess of a reasonable amount for funeral expenses. The fact that the operation of the Act was made retrospective in regard to policies which lapsed after 31st December, 1923, should be noticed in passing.

30. Under this Act the policy-holder is entitled to claim on application within one year from the date on which the last premium was paid either a free paid-up policy or a surrender value at his option, provided that not less than one year's premiums have been paid on the policy and that the policy is an endowment or endowment assurance issued either on the life of a child under the age of 10 years or as a "life of another" policy. It should be noted that this Act, unlike the 1923 Act, does not make the issue of a forfeiture notice a condition precedent to the grant of a paid-up policy or surrender value. The amount of the free paid-up policy is determined in accordance with the schedule to the Act by the proportionate paid-up policy method, whilst the surrender value of a policy is found by first ascertaining the free paid-up policy and then calculating 90 per cent. of the value of the free paid-up policy on the same basis as is prescribed by the 1923 Act, namely, the English Life Table No. 6 (Persons), with interest at 4 per cent.

CHAPTER IV

RULES OF REGISTERED FRIENDLY SOCIETIES

1. The rules of a friendly society are in some respects analogous to the articles of association of a company, inasmuch as they set forth the objects for which the society was established, the manner of convening meetings of members (corresponding to meetings of shareholders), rights of voting, and the conditions under which the committee of management (corresponding to the directors) hold office.

2. The First Schedule of the Friendly Societies Act, 1896, consists of a statement of the matters to be provided for by the rules of societies registered under the Act, and if the rules are based on the model rules prepared by the Registrar there is no likelihood of any statutory requirement not being met. It should be noted, however, that section 8 of the Industrial Assurance Act, 1923, requires that collecting friendly societies shall include in their rules the various sections of that Act referred to in the Second Schedule. The model rules, which are supplied free of charge, are extremely helpful and if followed save a great deal of the time, both of the society and the Registrar. It is of interest to note that in the case of one of the large orders, the Manchester Unity Friendly Society, the Registrar has approved standard rules both for districts and lodges, and these are printed as part of the general rules. The rules of an individual lodge may therefore take the very simple form of a few rules referring to points peculiar to it together with one rule in the following form:

The standard lodge rules of the Order set out in the general rules as added to or modified by these rules, shall be the rules of the lodge in the same manner and to the same extent as if they were contained in rules duly registered for the lodge.

A similar course can be followed by districts in regard to their rules, which are concerned primarily with the relations between the lodges forming the district. In all cases of inconsistency the district rules override the lodge rules, and the general rules of the order override the rules of the district and the lodge.

3. The various matters usually included in the rules may conveniently be divided into the following broad groups:

(i) Constitution and objects of the society and the investment of funds.

(ii) Terms upon which members are admitted, the payment of contributions and the receipt of benefit.

(iii) Appointment and removal of officers and committee of management, and their duties.

(iv) Administration, including audit and valuation and returns to the Registrar.

(v) Disputes and dissolution.

(vi) Interpretation and amendment of rules.

Detailed information on the subject-matter of groups (iii) to (vi) may be found in the *Guide Book of the Registry of Friendly Societies*, but the following notes may be useful in regard to groups (i) and (ii).

4. *Group (i). Constitution, objects and investment of funds.* The rules must state the objects of the society, and the operations of the society are definitely limited to the objects stated therein. It is essential to mention specifically in the rules all modes of investment which it is desired to adopt and which are not named in the Act. It is desirable, however, to mention also the latter class.

5. *Group (ii). Conditions of membership.* The matters dealt with in the second group of rules are very important and the valuer must give them special attention before commencing a valuation.

The conditions of membership vary considerably in different societies, but there is almost invariably a maximum age at entry into the society and in addition some societies exclude members resident in certain areas or employed in certain occupations, whilst other societies are restricted to members following a particular occupation. Prospective members are usually required to make a declaration concerning their medical history and in some cases the society requires in addition a medical report.

Contributions are usually paid either weekly, fortnightly, monthly or quarterly, and the fines and forfeitures to be imposed on any member and the consequences of non-payment of any subscription or fine must be provided for in the rules. A member is usually disqualified from the receipt of sickness benefit if his contributions are in arrear for more than a specified period, such as 13 weeks (or in some cases less), but a longer period, such as 26 weeks, is often allowed in the case of the death benefit. The continued non-payment of contributions for a further prescribed period, such as 26 weeks, entails the exclusion of the member from the society, and a member who wishes to reinstate himself during this period is almost invariably required to produce a satisfactory certificate of health.

The conditions governing the receipt of benefit vary widely, but, in order to give an indication of the type of conditions imposed by the rules, the following extracts are quoted from the standard lodge rules in operation in the Manchester Unity:

I. Every member of the lodge shall be entitled to benefit in case of sickness six calendar months after the date of admission, provided not less than six months' contributions have been paid by him.

The member usually becomes entitled to the full funeral benefit either immediately upon payment of the first contribution or after contributions have been paid for a short period such as one month.

II. A claimant for sick benefit must obtain the doctor's certificate which shall state the specific sickness from which the member is suffering, and shall, within 24 hours, forward the same to the secretary, together with the following declaration:

I, ..., residing at ...., by trade or profession ...., being prevented from following any occupation in consequence of sickness hereby claim the benefit of the lodge.

Signed ....
Date ....

This rule provides that before becoming entitled to sickness benefit the member must be unable to follow *any* occupation, but many lodges only insist upon the member's being unable to follow his usual occupation, and this is probably a more general condition.

III. The certificate must be renewed every four weeks, or oftener if required in the lodge special rules, so long as the member continues sick and claims the benefit except in special or chronic cases or where the member is a certified in-patient of a hospital. In either of the latter events the certificate shall be renewed at such times as may be decided upon by a resolution duly passed by the lodge.

IV. Upon a member declaring off the funds of the lodge he shall obtain the doctor's certificate, stating that he is able to resume his employment and shall deliver or forward it to the secretary within 24 hours.

V. Any member resuming his employment before he has obtained a certificate shall be liable to be fined in a sum not exceeding £1 or suffer such suspension as a summoned meeting of the lodge may think fit.

VI. Any member declaring off the sick fund, and again claiming the sick benefits of the lodge before the expiration of 52 weeks, shall only be entitled to the benefits he was then receiving, making the former and present one continued sickness, and shall be entitled to benefits accordingly.

VII. Should a member afflicted with a chronic or confirmed disease or infirmity declare off the funds without a certificate from a medical practitioner to the effect that he is cured, he shall in any subsequent declaration on the funds be treated as though the sickness had been continuous. Provided, however, that should the member declare off the funds having sufficiently recovered to be able to follow some occupation and remain off for three years he shall then be subject to the ordinary rules governing sickness benefit.

Sections VI and VII are very important as they regulate the off period. It will be appreciated that different conditions regarding the receipt of benefit may result in a material difference in the incidence of sickness claims, and this is a matter to be borne in mind when considering the results of a comparison of the actual sickness claims with those expected by any standard table.

VIII. Any member refusing to be seen by the doctor or sick visitor, or rendered incapable of following his employment by immoral or disorderly conduct, or by provoking or engaging in wanton quarrels or pursuits, or by accident arising from intoxication, shall not be entitled to sick benefit.

IX. A member claiming or in receipt of sickness or disablement benefit:

(a) shall obey the instructions of the doctor attending him;

(*b*) shall not be absent from home between the hours of 7 p.m. and 8 a.m. between the first day of October and the first day of March, and between 9 p.m. and 8 a.m. between the first day of March and the first day of October, and shall not be absent at any time without leaving word where he may be found, provided that one of the officers of the lodge upon the recommendation of the doctor may, if he thinks fit, exempt the member from the operation of this rule upon such conditions as he may impose;

(*c*) shall not leave the place where he resides without the consent of the secretary upon the recommendation of the doctor;

(*d*) shall not be guilty of conduct which is likely to retard his recovery;

(*e*) shall not follow any employment.

A member breaking these rules shall be fined a sum not exceeding ten shillings or in the case of repeated breaches of rules twenty shillings, or be liable to suspension of any benefit for a period not exceeding one year.

X. Any member imposing, or attempting to impose, on the funds by stating himself sick or incapable of following any employment, usual avocation, trade or calling, where he is able or actually doing so, or resuming his employment before having declared off in accordance with these rules, shall be expelled, or be fined a sum not exceeding £5 or suffer such suspension as a summoned meeting of the lodge may think fit.

CHAPTER V

METHODS OF SUBMITTING DATA FOR INVESTIGATION OF EXPERIENCE AND FOR VALUATION

1. The significance to be attached to a valuation must depend upon the degree of reliability to be placed upon the data, and it is therefore essential for the actuary to ensure at the outset that the particulars furnished by the society for valuation purposes shall be trustworthy. They should be presented in such a form as to afford him all the information he is likely to require in the course of his investigation.

2. Upon his appointment as valuer to a society, the actuary should obtain, in the first place, the following documents:

(i) A copy of the latest registered rules, including all partial amendments registered since the last complete amendment.

(ii) A copy of the last valuation report.

(iii) A copy of the annual return to the Registrar of Friendly Societies for each of the years since the date of the last valuation.

(iv) A copy of the printed accounts and balance sheets for the same years.

A detailed study of these documents should afford a sufficient general picture of the affairs of the society and should bring to light any features peculiar to the society and requiring special consideration. Assuming that the society is of moderate size, the next step is to ascertain—if possible by means of an interview with the secretary or other responsible official of the society—exactly in what form the society's own records are kept. It may even be advisable to visit the society's office in order to examine the records themselves, for in this way valuable information as to the reliability of the data may often be secured. In the case of some large societies it may be found possible to arrange for the work of compiling the data in a form suitable for valuation to be undertaken entirely by the secretary, acting under the instructions of the actuary, but in the case of the smaller societies the secretaries can hardly be expected to supply more than the fundamental information in respect of each contract in force. The more usual methods employed in the case of societies which grant sickness and other benefits are described in the following paragraphs.

3. The most simple method and the one usually employed in the case of small local societies where only one scale of benefits is in operation, is for the secretary to compile a roll of members giving the following particulars in respect of each member on the books at the valuation date:

    (i)   Name, initials or register number.

    (ii) Year of entry.

    (iii) Age at entry, either last birthday or next birthday according to the manner in which the rates of contributions are quoted in the rules.

    (iv) Annual contributions for benefits.

    (v) Annual contributions for management, distress and other purposes if separate from benefit contributions.

    (vi) Where the society has adopted a scheme prepared under section 72 of the National Insurance Act, 1911, the amount of the annual deduction from contributions allowed to members who availed themselves of the scheme.

    (vii) If a benefit payable on the death of a member's wife is provided, those members who have received this benefit are indicated. All other members whether married or single are assumed to be entitled to this benefit.

This information should be sufficient in the great majority of cases. The list can be extended to include any special features regarding which additional data may be required, but as simple a form as possible should be devised. It is not usual in the case of small local societies to ask for detailed information regarding the amount of sickness benefit drawn by individual members during the period under review, and the comparisons between the actual and expected sickness claims and the actual and expected deaths are generally made only in the aggregate. The "actual" figures in total are obtainable from the annual returns to the Registrar, and as the exposed to risk is usually taken as the mean of the assurances in force at successive valuation dates, frequently in quinary age groups the necessity for providing detailed information regarding the movements of membership is dispensed with. It sometimes happens that no records are available of the ages at entry and the years of entry of members admitted prior to a certain date, and in such cases the age last birthday at the valuation date is generally asked for.

The disadvantage of the method just described is that it generally involves a re-writing of the roll of members at successive valuations and a complete re-working of the valuation year of birth or any other figures inserted thereon by the actuary. In the case of small societies this is not a serious disadvantage, and sometimes in the case of the larger local societies the same roll of members can be used for one or possibly two additional valuations, if the exits since the last valuation date are crossed off and particulars of new contracts are added.

4. One of the large affiliated orders which previously had supplied information in this manner has now adopted the loose-leaf register system, a separate leaf (a specimen of which is reproduced on p. 36) being written for each member. The register is kept up to date by the district secretary, who merely extracts the leaves of those who have ceased membership and adds leaves for new members. It may be of interest to mention that although the average lodge contains only approximately 200 members, it has nevertheless been found economical in the case of this society to schedule the information by means of sorting and tabulating machines. The punched cards are made to serve at more than one valuation by punching thereon a membership or identification number in order to link them up with the membership leaves.

5. When a society is large enough to yield sufficient data to warrant a detailed investigation of the sickness and mortality experience, the method of writing a roll of members is quite unsuitable and the card system is much to be preferred, as the data may be sorted and tabulated with great facility in any manner required. A specimen card is reproduced on p. 37.

This card is designed solely for the purpose of the periodical actuarial investigations. Provision for the insertion of any other

Front of Leaf

		FOR ACTUARY'S USE.
	I.O.O.F., M.U.F.S.	

(Left vertical margin text:) No Management, Distress, or any Contribution other than that payable for Sickness, Death and Annuity Benefit must be shown on this side of the Form.

....**DISTRICT.**

LOYAL..**LODGE.** No. of Lodge................

Surname......................................Other Names.......................................Member's No................

Occupation...

Date of Birth..Joined { Initiation / Clearance ....Age last Birthday...........

Wife's Name...............................Date of Marriage................Date of Wife's Death.....................

Sickness Benefits cease at Age...........Contributions cease at Age...........Annuity commences at Age...........

BENEFITS. District Table No...................Scale.................... **CONTRIBUTIONS.**

In Sickness. First......weeks......s......d. per week	(1) Benefit Fund Contributions......s......d. every 4 wks.=£ : : per an.	
Next......weeks......s......d. „	(2) Amount Redeemed ......s......d. „ =£ : : „	
Next......weeks......s......d. „	(3) Net Amount Payable ....s......d. „ =£ : : „	
Next......weeks......s......d. „	(4) Reduction under Scheme......s......d. „ =£ : : „	
Thereafter ... .s......d. „	(5) Annuity contributions included in (1) above } ......s......d. „ =£ : : „	
Annuity com'cing at Age...... ......s......d. „		
Amount Re-assured with D.F.F.	Non-Returnable/Returnable at Death before age..........	
At Death. Member £ : : £ : :	If the D.F.F. is supported by Contributions or Poundage.	
Wife £ : : £ . :	(6) Contributions to D.F.F. ......s......d. per Quarter =£ : : per an.	
Date of exit..	Rate of Poundage to D.F.F......................	
Cause of exit..		

Back of Leaf

LODGE ———— **DISTRICT** **WIDOW AND ORPHAN FUND.** Date of Joining............................Age last Birthday.........

Benefits...............................Contributions......s......d. per......................=£ : : per an.

Notes of Increase or Reduction of Benefits overleaf.

Date........................ Nature of Alteration...

„ .... „ „ ....

„ .... „ „ ....

„ .... „ „ ....

REMARKS :—

information which may be required by the secretary can easily be made by a slight re-drafting of the card. One card could in fact be drafted to serve the purpose of both a valuation card and a record card, but, as the cards are in the hands of the actuary for two or three months and during that time reference to them by the society would be both difficult and irritating, it is preferable and more usual to have separate cards. On the front of the card are the particulars which the society obtains at the member's admission, and spaces for the date and cause of exit and the date of the pay-

...................................F.S.				
Mem s. No.................Table......................				
Name..				
Occupation..........................Sex............				

Date of	D.	M.	Y.		Age n.b.d. at entry
Birth....					
Entry....					
Exit.....					

Cause of exit..

Date of wife's death.......................................

Amount of full sick pay per week	£.	s.	d.
Contribution per annum			

Remarks

Val⁰ yr. of bth........ Full sick pay............						
Record of sickness claims.						
Year	Full.		Half.		Quarter.	
	W	D	W	D	W	D
1926						

※The lower half of the card can be
suitably modified for other benefits.

ment of the wife's funeral benefit. The rectangular "box" on the right-hand side of the card is reserved for the use of the actuary. The back of the card contains a record of the number of weeks' sickness benefit received by the member during the successive years, at each rate of pay. Instead of weeks of sickness, the actual cost of the claims at each rate of pay may be inserted or both weeks and cost may be given, but it is more usual to ask for weeks of sickness, information as to the cost being obtained, if required, by scheduling the claims separately under each separate rate of full pay. The card does not contain the details of each separate claim for full or reduced pay during each year, but only the total of the separate claims at each rate of pay during any one year. If information is required as to claims arising in respect of accidents, as distinct from ordinary sickness, it can conveniently be inserted on the card by using a differently coloured ink. In some societies, particularly the old-established county societies, a separate contribution is paid for each benefit, and it has been found more convenient to have a card written in respect of each assurance for which a separate contribution is payable, the cards relating to the same member being correlated, if necessary, by means of a note in the space for remarks. The few alterations of contract which arise can be made in red ink and an explanatory note added.

One great advantage of the card system is that the cards may be made to serve for a number of quinquennia. The card contains for all practical purposes a complete and permanent record of each assurance taken out with the society, and when the time comes for the cards to be re-written, say once in 25 years, all the information on the old card, apart from the sickness record, can be transferred to the new. In order to keep the cards up to date, it is merely necessary to write cards for new members, to enter up particulars of sickness claims, to give effect to alterations in the contracts and to write off those who cease membership. One point of practical importance should be mentioned. In order to make the cards last for as long a period as possible the secretary may wish to have the first column on the back of the card left blank and only enter thereon the years in which the individual members actually make a claim for sickness benefit. This would, however, detract seriously from the practical advantages of the method and, despite the inconvenience of having to introduce an entirely new set of cards at one date, the years should be printed on the cards in order that the claims for any one particular year may appear in the same relative position on all cards.

6. A method sometimes adopted in the case of larger societies is for the secretary, acting under the instructions of the actuary, to

supply the data in tabular form. The actuary is thus relieved of all the preliminary work in connection with the sorting and tabulating of the data, the schedules supplied by the secretary being in the final form described in the later chapters on experience and valuation. This method can only be employed where it is possible to rely implicitly upon the officials of the society, but, once the method of procedure has been established, the system works well. Arrangements should be made when such a scheme is inaugurated for the actuary to inspect the progress of the work at the various stages.

7. A further method which is sometimes employed involves the use of dual punch cards and of sorting and tabulating machines. On about one-quarter of the card are written the usual particulars of the assurance, and such of these as are required for the investigation are punched on the remainder of the card.

8. In whatever form the data are supplied they should first of all be examined by means of samples, particular care being taken to see that effect has been given to any alterations of rules which may have affected the amount of the contributions or benefits. The contributions paid by new members should be checked with the rules and, where the valuation particulars have been entirely re-written from one valuation to the next, the information as to year of entry, age at entry and contribution should be checked, in a number of instances chosen at random, with the corresponding information furnished on the preceding occasion. It may be found, for instance, that a new secretary has, in error, supplied the age last birthday at entry whilst his predecessor gave an age next birthday at entry, an alteration which would have a considerable effect upon the valuation result if it were not detected.

9. Methods by which the data may be scheduled in the form required for the investigation, as indicated in the chapters on experience and valuation, may now be considered. The main classification is according to the age attained at the valuation date. It is usual to record the valuation year of birth, which remains constant throughout the duration of the assurance, rather than the valuation age,

which varies at each valuation date. The following are the more usual methods of obtaining the valuation year of birth, the first being the one most commonly used:

(i) If the year of entry and the age at entry are employed, the valuation year of birth is the calendar year of entry minus the age next birthday at entry, the assumption being that the age next birthday at entry is attained at the end of the year of entry.

(ii) If the actual date of birth is employed, the valuation year of birth for a valuation as at 31st December is the calendar year in which falls the 31st December nearest to the actual date of birth. If the valuation date is 30th June the actual calendar year of birth is also the valuation year of birth.

(iii) Sometimes only the year of birth and not the actual date of birth is available, and the valuation may then be made at half-ages on the assumption that births take place on the average in the middle of the year. The valuation year of birth is then identical with the actual year of birth and the valuation age is equal to (year of valuation − year of birth + $\frac{1}{2}$).

If the data are supplied on cards the information required for the actual valuation can quite conveniently be listed under valuation year of birth, either by hand or by means of machinery, and the totals at each valuation age obtained. It may sometimes be found convenient also to list the membership number so that, if necessary, the schedules can be used at a subsequent valuation by crossing off those cases which have ceased membership and adding the new assurances. In the case of the larger societies it may be found possible to obtain the particulars for one valuation from those supplied at the previous valuation date by dealing only with the "ons" and "offs".

10. For the purpose of constructing the exposed to risk, cards relating to new entrants, exits and existing should be sorted and scheduled as indicated in the next chapter. The next process is to obtain the actual weeks of sickness (or cost of sickness as the case may be) arranged in such a form as to enable a comparison to be made between the actual and the expected. The data are then scheduled in the following form:

Valua-tion year of birth	Actual sickness claims at full pay rate in year												
	1926			1927			...	1930			1926–30		
	Age*	wks	days	Age*	wks	days		Age*	wks	days	Age*	wks	days
1910	15			16									
1909	16			17									
1908	17			18									

* The age is the valuation age at 31st December preceding year of claim. In practice it is unnecessary to insert age columns for the individual years.

The age at claim is obtained by deducting the valuation year of birth from the year of claim minus 1, and an upward diagonal cast gives the total claims at each age. The number of cards upon which a claim appears should be tabulated in a similar manner if it is thought necessary to investigate, in addition, the proportion of members sick. Such an investigation can be of considerable assistance in determining to what extent excessive sickness may be attributed to the number of claimants, or to the average duration of claims.

The advantage to be secured from scheduling the claims under year of claim is that the claims of each separate year may be examined in conjunction with any special conditions which have prevailed in that year and which may have affected the experience, and thus a more correct interpretation of the character of the experience may be obtained.

11. The most convenient method in practice of scheduling these particulars is to employ sorting and tabulating machines. The punched card shows the valuation year of birth, the calendar year of claim, the rate of full sick pay, the period of sickness in which the claim occurred, and the number of weeks and days. A separate card is punched for each item at each rate of pay shown on the valuation card, including of course all claims by members who have ceased membership for any reason during the period under investigation. The cards are first sorted under calendar year of claim and are then sub-sorted under valuation year of birth, the aggregate number of weeks and days being tabulated in the form shown.

Separate tabulations should be made for each separate rate of full pay if a comparison is required of the actual and expected cost of benefits, unless the data card also contains the cash amount of benefit received. It is sometimes desirable to examine the experience in separate groups according to the amount of full sick pay assured, and in this case also it is necessary to make separate tabulations of the actual claims. The only alternative to the use of sorting and tabulating machines is that of scheduling by hand (or by means of a tabulating and adding machine) the actual claims either under valuation year of birth and year of claim or under age at claim (if this information is inserted on the card against each year of claim). As each item appearing on the card would have to be separately scheduled this method is exceedingly laborious. The disadvantage of sorting and tabulating machines is that they are expensive to instal, but as there are facilities for obtaining at a reasonable cost the assistance of these machines for a particular investigation this difficulty can easily be overcome. The actual claims for accident or unemployment benefits can be scheduled in exactly the same manner and the punched card can generally be adapted to meet any special circumstances. In fact one of the great advantages of the system is its elasticity.

12. When all the data for both the valuation and the experience have been scheduled, it is essential to apply as many independent checks as possible, and for this purpose a certain amount of useful information may be obtained by analysing the figures contained in the annual returns to the Registrar. The following checks should be made:

(i) The numbers, as obtained from the cards, of new entrants, exits and existing members should be compared for each year of the investigation with the numbers given in the annual returns. Although in the case of the larger societies precise agreement cannot always be obtained, reasonably close agreement should be secured.

(ii) The total annual contribution income as obtained from the valuation schedules should be compared with the amount of contributions actually received during the preceding calendar year, allowance being made for arrears (particulars of which should be found in the annual returns) and for changes of membership during the year. A further check on the total contributions for benefits received during the period under review may be obtained by comparing this amount with an "expected" amount based upon the mean between the annual incomes shown by the last and present valuation schedules, allowance being made for arrears and for abnormal changes of membership.

(iii) The actual amount received by way of interest during each year should be checked by comparing it with the interest income expected to be derived from the investments, allowance being made for the effect of any changes of investments made during the year and for the incidence of income tax. Frequently tax deducted at source in one year is not recovered until the following year, nor is credit taken in the balance sheet for the amount recoverable. In the case of smaller societies it occasionally happens that income tax is not, in fact, being reclaimed. In such circumstances the attention of the officials should be drawn to the omission and they should be informed of their right to reclaim in respect of the last six years.

(iv) The actual sickness claims as totalled from the data cards should be compared with the corresponding items in the annual returns for individual years. Payments made by way of death benefits should be checked approximately by reference to the number of deaths and the average amount of benefit. A similar check can be obtained on the annuity payments.

(v) The distribution of the membership according to age should be compared with that shown by the last valuation schedules.

CHAPTER VI

EXPERIENCE AND BASIS
OF VALUATION

1. Before the basis of valuation can be determined it is necessary to examine the society's experience. A registered friendly society is required to submit a valuation of its assets and liabilities not less frequently than once in every five years, and although a few of the larger societies, chiefly the centralized or semi-centralized societies, are valued regularly at intervals of one or three years, in the majority of cases the inter-valuation period is five years. As the valuation date is usually the 31st December, the period is composed of complete calendar years, and the calendar year method of examining the experience is therefore eminently suitable.

2. Frequently the experience of one or two previous quinquennia is already available and, in the important decisions which have to be taken in regard to the valuation basis, consideration should be given to previous experience as well as to that of the quinquennium just completed. This is particularly necessary if the last valuation period was one during which unsettled economic conditions prevailed. On the other hand, however, if there have been alterations in the rules during the quinquennium which were of such a nature as to alter apparently the character of the experience it will be necessary to exercise caution in deciding upon the weight to be attached to the past experience. In the case of small societies it is usually sufficient to take the mean of the numbers at risk at the beginning and end of the period as indicated in Chapter v, paragraph 3.

3. In the following paragraphs the symbols employed are:

b_x, cases existing at the last valuation date.

n_x, new entrants during the quinquennium.

e_x, existing cases at the valuation date.

d_x, deaths during the quinquennium.

w_x, withdrawals during the quinquennium.

$^d\mathrm{E}_x$, exposed to risk of mortality.

$^w\mathrm{E}_x$, ,, ,, withdrawal.

$^s\mathrm{E}_x$, ,, ,, sickness.

The first process is to insert on the valuation card the valuation year of birth, which is usually obtained by deducting the age next birthday at admission from the year of admission. Once this information has been recorded, the age at successive valuations is readily obtainable.

The next process is to sort the cards into two groups:

      (I) the members existing at the valuation date,

and   (II) the exits during the inter-valuation period.

These groups are best scheduled entirely separately throughout.

4. Dealing first with group (I), the cards will be sub-sorted into two groups:

      (a) cases existing at the last valuation date (b_x),

and   (b) new entrants during the quinquennium (n_x).

The valuation date will be taken as 31st December, 1930, and it will be assumed that the previous valuation was made as at 31st December, 1925. Group (a) will be scheduled under valuation year of birth, the ages at entry into the experience being obtained by deducting the valuation year of birth from 1925, and the ages at exit by deducting from 1930. As the cases comprised within group (b) will have been exposed to risk for fractional periods of a year it is necessary to make an assumption in dealing with their duration of exposure. On the usual assumption that the dates of entry are equally spread over the year of entry (the accuracy of the assumption should of course be tested) either of two further assumptions can be made:

(i) That all members enter in the middle of the year, in which case the duration of exposure is the curtate duration plus half a year in every case and the formula can be constructed so as to make the necessary allowance for the half-year;

(ii) That the date of entry is the nearest 31st December to the actual date of entry.

The second method has the advantage over the first that the age at the assumed date of entry and the duration of exposure will be integral. All that is necessary in this case is to insert on the card a "valuation year of entry", being the year in which the nearest

31st December to the actual date of entry occurs, and to schedule the cards as under:

New Entrants during the Quinquennium—Group (I) (*b*)

Valuation year of birth	Valuation year of entry						Age x	Total aged x at entry	Total aged x at valuation date
	1925	1926	1927	1928	1929	1930			
1910						3	20	34	
1909					7	2	21		
1908				8	5	5	22		
1907			6	6	6	6	23		
1906		6	5	3	4	3	24		
1905	4	7	6	2	7	6	25		32

A cast of the numbers across the diagonal gives the number of members who entered at each age at entry, i.e. n_x, and the horizontal cross-cast gives the number according to the valuation year of birth, and hence the number at each age at the valuation date, i.e. e_x. Thus the diagonal cast underlined shows 34 members to have entered at age 20 and the horizontal cast shows 32 to be the number of existing members at the valuation date at age 25.

5. In scheduling group (II), the exits during the inter-valuation period, the first process will be to sort them into sub-groups according to the mode of exit. Each sub-group will then have to be tabulated twice—firstly according to age at entry into the experience—and for this purpose the method followed will be the same as that described for the existing members (two groups being obtained, i.e. b_x and n_x)—and secondly as exits from the experience. The period of exposure given to exits will depend upon which of the rates are being investigated. Thus, if the rates of mortality are being examined, the exits by death must be given a full year's exposure in the year of death, whilst, if the rates of withdrawal are being investigated, the exits by death must be given, on the average, one-half a year's exposure in the year of death. It is convenient, in practice, to adopt a uniform method for all causes of exit and to schedule the cards as under. The correct periods of exposure are ensured in the construction of the formula for the exposed to risk.

Cause of Exit...

Valuation year of birth	Actual year of exit					Age at 31st December preceding year of exit x	Total at age x at exit
	1926	1927	1928	1929	1930		
1909					1	20	4
1908				—			
1907			2				
1906		—					
1905	1						
etc.							

The diagonal cast then gives the numbers at the same age at the 1st January of the year of exit: thus the diagonal cast indicated by the underlining shows four cases as having dropped out of the experience at age 20.

6. The last process is to amalgamate the various groups of b_x (i.e. those from the schedules for existing members and those from the schedules for the exits for each of the different causes of exit) and similarly to combine the n_x into another group.

7. If the experience is being examined with regard to mortality, withdrawal and sickness, it is necessary to calculate three separate columns of exposed to risk, but the usual procedure is to obtain the exposed to risk for mortality first and to make such adjustments to it as are indicated by the formulas in order to obtain the exposures for withdrawal and sickness. In the construction of the formulas for the exposed to risk, account must be taken of the conditions governing the receipt of benefits. Suppose that the rules of the society provide for:

   (i) immediate death benefit at entry;

   (ii) a waiting period of six months for sickness benefit;

   (iii) suspension of sickness benefit if more than 13 weeks' contributions are in arrear;

(iv) suspension from all benefits, including the death benefit, if more than 26 weeks' contributions are owing; and

(v) unless arrears are paid within the next 26 weeks and such evidence of good health is furnished as the rules may require, complete exclusion from the society when contributions are one year in arrear.

It is important to ascertain the method adopted by the secretary of the society of recording the date of lapse, as some secretaries insert the date after which no benefit is payable whilst others insert the date of complete exclusion. It will be assumed that the former method has been adopted. It is preferable, in fact, to request that this method should be followed, whatever the system adopted by the secretary for the purpose of the society's internal record may be, as, otherwise, adjustments will have to be made. The formulas will then be, on the assumption that the ages have been fixed in accordance with the preceding paragraphs:

(i) For mortality

$$^dE_x = {}^dE_{x-1} + b_x + n_x - d_{x-1} - \tfrac{1}{2}(w_x + w_{x-1}) - e_x.$$

(ii) For withdrawal

$$^wE_x = {}^wE_{x-1} + b_x + n_x - \tfrac{1}{2}(d_x + d_{x-1}) - w_{x-1} - e_x.$$

(iii) For sickness

$$^sE_x = {}^sE_{x-1} + b_x + \tfrac{1}{2}(n_x + n_{x-1}) - (\tfrac{3}{4}w_x + \tfrac{1}{4}w_{x-1}) - \tfrac{1}{2}(d_x + d_{x-1}) - e_x.$$

8. A discussion of the general theory of exposed to risk formulas is beyond the scope of this book, but it may be useful to include the following demonstration of the accuracy of the type of formula here employed. Omitting for the sake of simplicity all causes of exit other than death and taking into account a two-year period, namely 1926–27, the exposed to risk at age x for mortality, ^dE_x, can be built up as follows, the prefixes to the symbols denoting the year (fixed in accordance with the preceding paragraphs) of entry and exit and the symbols themselves being as defined in paragraph 3. For example $_{26}n_x$ denotes the new entrants for valuation year of entry 1926.

Year	No. exposed to risk at age x
1926	$b_x + {}_{26}n_x$
1927	$b_{x-1} + {}_{27}n_x + {}_{26}n_{x-1} - {}_{26}d_{x-1}$

Thus $E_x = (b_x + b_{x-1}) + {}_{26}n_x + {}_{27}n_x + {}_{26}n_{x-1} - {}_{26}d_{x-1}$.

Similarly

$$E_{x-1} = (b_{x-1} + b_{x-2}) + {}_{26}n_{x-1} + {}_{27}n_{x-1} + {}_{26}n_{x-2} - {}_{26}d_{x-2},$$

and

$$E_x - E_{x-1} = (b_x - b_{x-2}) + {}_{26}n_x + {}_{27}n_x - {}_{27}n_{x-1} - {}_{26}n_{x-2} - {}_{26}d_{x-1} + {}_{26}d_{x-2}.$$

But $e_x = b_{x-2} + {}_{26}n_{x-2} + {}_{27}n_{x-1} - {}_{26}d_{x-2} - {}_{27}d_{x-1},$

therefore

$$E_x - E_{x-1} = b_x + ({}_{26}n_x + {}_{27}n_x) - ({}_{26}d_{x-1} + {}_{27}d_{x-1}) - e_x,$$

i.e. $$E_x = E_{x-1} + b_x + n_x - d_{x-1} - e_x.$$

9. The following notes may help to elucidate the special points in the actual formulas for the case under consideration:

(i) In the formulas for mortality, a full year's exposure to risk of death is given for deaths by deducting d_{x-1} instead of d_x. The withdrawals are at risk on the average for six months during the year of withdrawal, and the correct total exposure is obtained by regarding one-half of the number as having withdrawn on 1st January of the year of withdrawal, and the remaining half on the 31st December of that year. This is achieved in the formula by deducting $\frac{1}{2}w_x$ and $\frac{1}{2}w_{x-1}$ respectively. Only those cases where a death benefit has been paid or is payable should be recorded as deaths. In fact as no benefit is payable at the death of a member whose contributions are six months in arrear, the society probably has no further record after the six months have elapsed.

(ii) In the formula for withdrawal, the deaths scheduled at age x (d_x) are re-distributed, on the assumption that the dates of death are equally spread over the year, as $\frac{1}{2}d_x$ at the beginning and $\frac{1}{2}d_x$ at the end of the year. One-half of the number of deaths, i.e. those assumed to have died at the end of the year, may then be given exposure to risk of withdrawal for a full year and the other half no exposure. Accordingly the number of deaths to be taken out of the exposed to risk at age x is $\frac{1}{2}d_{x-1} + \frac{1}{2}d_x$, the group $\frac{1}{2}d_{x-1}$ obtaining a full year's exposure and the group $\frac{1}{2}d_x$ no exposure.

(iii) In the formula for sickness, two points require comment. The new entrant, who by the method of scheduling is assumed to enter at exact age x, is not at risk until age $x + \frac{1}{2}$ is reached (owing to the waiting period) and accordingly one-half of the entrants are brought into the exposure at age x and one-half at age $x+.1$, the group $\frac{1}{2}n_{x-1}$ representing the number whose entry into the experience was deferred until the end of the year. The withdrawals are only at risk on the average for the first three months of the year of withdrawal, since, if the date of withdrawal be assumed to be the middle of the actual year of withdrawal, they must be taken out of the experience as at a date three months earlier. The number at age x should thus be exposed for $\frac{1}{4}$ year from age x, and this is effected on balance by giving $\frac{1}{4}$ of the number a full year's exposure from age x (by deducting $\frac{1}{4}w_x$ in the formula for ${}^sE_{x+1}$), and $\frac{3}{4}$ of the number no exposure in the year of age x to $x+1$ (deducting $\frac{3}{4}w_x$ in the formula for ${}^sE_x$).

Assuming that the exposed to risk for mortality, ${}^dE_x$, has been calculated, the exposed to risk for withdrawal can be obtained by means of the formula

$$ {}^wE_x = {}^dE_x + \tfrac{1}{2}w_x - \tfrac{1}{2}d_x, $$

since

$$ {}^wE_x = \Sigma\,[b_x + n_x - w_{x-1} - \tfrac{1}{2}(d_x + d_{x-1}) - e_x] $$

summed for all ages up to and including x, and

$$ {}^dE_x = \Sigma\,[b_x + n_x - d_{x-1} - \tfrac{1}{2}(w_x + w_{x-1}) - e_x] $$

similarly summed, and therefore

$$ {}^wE_x - {}^dE_x = \tfrac{1}{2}w_x - \tfrac{1}{2}d_x. $$

In a similar fashion it can be shown that

$$ {}^sE_x = {}^dE_x - \tfrac{1}{2}n_x - \tfrac{1}{2}d_x - \tfrac{1}{4}w_x. $$

10. The working sheet would be headed as follows:

Column (1) Age x.	Column (8) $g_x = (5) + (6) + (7)$.
,, (2) b_x.	,, (9) $h_x = (4) - (8)$.
,, (3) n_x.	,, (10) ${}^x\Sigma h_x = {}^dE_x$.
,, (4) $f_x = (2) + (3)$.	,, (11) $\frac{1}{2}(w_x - d_x)$.
,, (5) d_{x-1}.	,, (12) ${}^wE_x = (10) + (11)$.
,, (6) $\frac{1}{2}(w_x + w_{x-1})$.	,, (13) $\frac{1}{2}n_x + \frac{1}{2}d_x + \frac{1}{4}w_x$.
,, (7) e_x.	,, (14) ${}^sE_x = (10) - (13)$.

Note ${}^x\Sigma h_x$ is obtained by summing column (9) from the youngest age down to and including age x.

11. In the comparison of the expected sickness and the actual sickness, the trend of the experience throughout the period should also be examined, and it is sometimes useful to construct an exposed to risk for each year of the quinquennium. Although at first sight it may seem that this is likely to be a lengthy process, the following working sheet shows that the work can be quickly performed. New entrants and exits are scheduled under valuation year of entry or actual year of exit as before, but no cross or diagonal casts are required. In this case the working sheet would be as under:

Column (1) Age x.
   ,,   (2) b_x 1925.
   ,,   (3) n_x 1925.
   ,,   (4) (2) + (3).
   ,,   (5) w_x 1925.

Column (6) d_x 1925.
   ,,   (7) (5) + (6).
   ,,   (8) (4) $-\frac{1}{2}$(5) $= {}^d E_x$.
   ,,   (9) (4) $-$ (7) $= b_x$ 1926.

and so on for the following years.

Although the functions ${}^w E_x$ and ${}^s E_x$ can be obtained from ${}^d E_x$ by an adjustment, it is probably almost as convenient to calculate each of them afresh.

12. The exposed to risk having been ascertained, it is a simple matter to calculate the number of "expected" deaths, and, if a rate of secession has been employed, the number of "expected" withdrawals, and the "expected" weeks of sick pay in the various periods of sickness. The "expected" should always be calculated in the first instance upon the basis of the rates employed in the last valuation in order that the financial effect of the actual experience during the quinquennium may be determined. In the paragraphs which follow, each element of the basis is discussed separately, but it is essential to remember that the valuation basis should be considered as a whole. Where margins exist in respect of some of the elements the action taken as a result of an adverse experience in the case of one of the others need not be as stringent as if no such margin existed.

13. It is as well to mention that changes in the valuation basis are undesirable unless there is satisfactory evidence that a change is necessary. On the other hand, however, it is very important to recognize any indications that a change in the basis will become necessary in a subsequent valuation and it is wise, in practice, to make partial provision for an impending change of basis by setting up a special reserve in the valuation balance sheet.

Thus, if the mortality experience for the quinquennium should show that the percentage of actual to "expected" deaths was low, and that even when the experience of the 10 years preceding the valuation date was taken into account the percentage was still below 100, and if the alternative to the table at present employed is one showing rates of mortality too light to justify their adoption in the present valuation but likely to be appropriate in the course of a decade in view of the progressive improvement which is taking place, it would be reasonable to employ the existing mortality table, provided that a special reserve was introduced with the object of making partial provision for the increased reserves which will be necessitated by the change of basis at a subsequent valuation. The student may not realize how great a strain may be imposed, where sickness benefits are payable throughout life, by the adoption of lighter rates of mortality. It is much better to make provision gradually for such a revision by increasing the special reserve in stages until the change is fully justified, as it can then be made without a violent repercussion upon the financial position of the society. This method has the advantage that instead of surpluses shown at one or two successive valuations being followed by a considerable deficiency at the next, which would be the case if, as is likely, the surpluses in the meantime were appropriated, the successive valuations would probably show the society to be solvent throughout. It is worth while to remember that although the actuary may recommend in his report that a surplus should be carried forward unappropriated, it is often entirely within the power of the members to absorb the surplus by an increase of benefits. Happily those responsible for the management of friendly societies are paying more and more attention to the advice of the actuary, but a disclosed surplus which cannot be taken advantage of by the members often causes considerable difficulty for the officials of the society. Much of what has been written here applies with particular force to the smaller societies, as, in the case of the larger societies, there is always the alternative of revising the valuation basis at more frequent intervals, using in this case rates of mortality deduced from the society's own experience. It is not practicable, however, to adopt this course in the case of the smaller societies, not only because there would not be sufficient data but also, probably, on account of the cost of the preparation of the necessary valuation factors. The question naturally arises as to whether a society should be valued on the basis of its own experience or by means of a standard table. The essential condition for the former alternative is that the membership should be large enough to yield, in not too long a period, sufficient data to give reliable results. When rates are based on the society's own experience care must be exercised to see that a normal period is chosen.

14. In practically all the smaller societies, and also in many of the larger ones, the element of withdrawal is ignored in framing the valuation basis. Only in cases where there is a decided and consistent experience of withdrawals in comparatively large numbers, should rates of withdrawal be introduced, and even then it is wiser, if the financial position of the society permits, to omit them. The effect of their omission will be that higher reserves than might be held to be strictly necessary will be made but correspondingly larger surpluses will be disclosed at subsequent valuations. In any case, where rates of withdrawal are employed, a conservative estimate must be made and rates approximating to one-half of those actually experienced should be regarded as· the maximum. An important point to remember in connection with the withdrawal experience is that rates of withdrawal depend very largely upon duration of membership, and if, as is usual, an aggregate valuation is made, the rates incorporated in the valuation basis should cease at a comparatively early age. Before the rates of withdrawal are fixed, the experience of members of not less than five years' duration of membership should be examined. The employment of rates of withdrawal is fully dealt with in Watson's *Lectures on Friendly Society Finance*, pp. 39–45, and in *J.I.A.* Vol. XLIV, p. 194.

If withdrawal rates are introduced into the basis it must not be overlooked that benefits (if any) payable upon withdrawal must be valued as liabilities.

15. The standard tables of sickness rates now in general use are based on the Manchester Unity 1893–97 Experience (A. W. Watson's tables), and only in special circumstances would basic sickness rates deduced from the society's own experience be employed. This does not mean, however, that modifications of the standard tables may not be necessary. On the contrary, the sickness experience of the society must be fully examined in order to determine to what extent such modifications are required.

The actual experience should first be examined separately in age groups for each period for which a different rate of sickness benefit is payable. It is not unusual to find that whereas the number of actual weeks of sickness at the full pay rate may be considerably in excess of the expectation, the actual weeks at the reduced rates of pay are approximately equal to or even less than the standard, and inasmuch as an excess of sickness at the full rate of benefit is much more costly than a like excess at the reduced rates the necessity for detailed examination will be apparent. The financial effect may be very well displayed by converting both the actual and expected weeks of sickness into equivalent weeks of full pay, when a comparison of the resultant totals of actual and expected will afford an indication of how far an excess at one period may be offset by a defect in another.

In the case of a society which has a wide range of scales of full pay it is desirable to examine the experience on a cost basis in order to ascertain whether the experience differs to any material extent according to the rate of full benefit. A full examination could be made by the same method as has been outlined for the examination of the sickness experience in regard to weeks of sickness, by taking into account units of 1s. of full sick pay instead of members, but it would probably be sufficient for the purpose in view to calculate the expected cost of sickness by reference to the mean of the number of shillings in force at the last and the present valuation dates. If the percentage of actual to expected cost was substantially higher than the corresponding percentage for weeks of sickness, an investigation should be made into the experience under the several rates of full pay and, if the results were such as to call for differentiation in the loadings, separate valuations would have to be made.

Usually, when a loading is necessary, it is sufficient to increase the sickness values by a constant percentage or by percentages varying according to periods of sickness, but sometimes it is necessary to load separately in each of three or four broad age groups.

16. The subject of select sickness rates is discussed by Harvey in an appendix to his paper (*J.I.A.* Vol. LIV, p. 180), where he shows how the select rates used in the calculation of transfer values under the National Health Insurance Scheme were framed. The assumption was that a member who wished to transfer would not be sick at the date of transfer and accordingly, if x was his present age, he would not be suffering at age $x + t$ from sickness of greater duration than t. On this hypothesis the deductions to be made from the aggregate rates were calculated and the diagram shows very clearly the method employed. Special attention is drawn in the paper to the fact that "these select rates are not select in the ordinary sense, i.e. they are not rates resulting from the experience of medically selected lives". In the case of a friendly society no allowance would ordinarily be made for this form of selection but special circumstances, such as a very large influx of new members, might render it desirable to give effect to selection in the valuation basis.

17. The other element in the basis, the rate of interest, also requires careful consideration. The average rate of interest earned for each year and for the valuation period has to be calculated for the purposes of the form F 40 by means of the usual formula:

$$\text{Rate of interest} = \frac{2I}{A+B-I}.$$

This calculation is made upon the basis of the total funds, the object being to ascertain whether the society's funds are reasonably well invested. It is necessary also for the purpose of fixing the valuation rate of interest to know the average rate of interest credited to the benefit fund. If the actual interest received has not been allocated correctly, or if any fund has a claim to be credited with interest at a specified rate regardless of the actual yield, the rate credited to the benefit fund may differ from that earned upon the total funds. If it has been decided to set up a reserve in the valuation balance sheet for depreciation, due allowance should be made for this when calculating the rate of interest credited to the benefit fund. In calculating the rate of interest, only net interest should be taken into account, deductions being made from the gross interest and rents for all charges such as the cost of collection, outgoings on property, commission or trustees' expenses, or appreciation wrongly included as interest. The annual return to the Registrar has a space provided for an investments account and statement, and where this is correctly completed no difficulty should arise. In some cases, however, items of expenditure which should properly form a charge on interest income are debited to the management fund, and in such cases the attention of the society may well be drawn to the proper method of dealing with them, particularly if there is difficulty in meeting the ordinary expenses of management from the management fund.

It is desirable, whenever possible, to retain a margin between the rate of interest earned and the valuation rate. It should be remembered that the contracts now being entered into by the younger members may continue for as long as 50 years or more, and that although the rate being earned at the valuation date may be high, the market rate may fall to a much lower level long before the contracts now in force have terminated. The strain involved in the reduction of the valuation rate may be very considerable and an increase in the valuation rate, involving, as possibly it will, a reduction at a later date, should only be made if there is a large margin of interest or other substantial source of surplus such as a light sickness experience, and not always even then. A margin between the rate assumed and the rate earned is a valuable source of surplus, and may provide just enough in a particular quinquennium to counteract the effect of an adverse fluctuation in the sickness experience, with the result that the society would remain solvent instead, possibly, of being thrown into deficiency.

It must be borne in mind that as, in general, there is no recognized system in friendly society finance analogous to the reversionary bonus system of life assurance practice, there is no necessity for preserving an interest margin as a means of providing for the cost of bonuses at subsequent valuations. The necessity for retaining a margin arises rather from the need of securing, as far as it is possible to do so, that the members shall receive throughout their lifetime their basic benefits, and as in the case of a society granting sickness benefits, in contra-distinction to a life office, an improvement in the mortality experience is, as a rule, financially adverse, a margin in the rate of interest serves as a valuable safeguard.

18. The calculation of rates of contribution for a new society generally presents difficulties, as it is only in rare instances, such as that of a new society formed in conjunction with an old-established undertaking, that it is possible to obtain data on which to base estimates of what the future experience of the society is likely to be. Having given the area in which the society is to operate and the class of lives which the society intends to recruit, one can usually select a mortality table which appears to be appropriate. The student will have already gathered that it is of fundamental importance that the table so selected should not overestimate the mortality likely to be experienced. In fixing the rate of interest the same considerations as have just been discussed in paragraph 17 arise. If in practice it is found that the society is able to secure a higher rate of interest than that upon which the contributions are based, no injustice to the members need result, as any surpluses disclosed at successive valuations could be distributed for the benefit of members. It is in connection with the provision for future sickness claims that the greatest difficulty arises and, whilst an impression of what the sickness experience is likely to be can be formed from the type of life it is proposed to admit into the society, it is clear that the society must, to some extent, "buy" its own experience.

CHAPTER VII

VALUATION

1. The work of valuation may be divided into two parts: (i) the construction of the necessary factors, if these have not been published, and (ii) the actual process of valuation, including the necessary overhead checks to test as far as possible the general accuracy of the results. It should be understood that much of this chapter applies only to large societies. It would not, indeed, be possible to carry out some of the processes in the case of small societies owing to the lack of the requisite data. Even if the data were obtainable they would be too fragmentary to justify either the amount of work involved or the results.

2. The fundamental annual rates having been determined and the rate of interest decided, the first step will be to obtain the usual annuity and assurance functions. These do not require any comment and the next process is the construction of the sickness factors.

It has already been mentioned that it will usually be satisfactory to make any loading which may be necessary in the form of a constant percentage addition for all ages, and consequently the standard sickness rates may generally be used as a basis. In cases, however, where there is a marked divergence at certain periods of life from the standard rates, other methods should be adopted. Two alternatives are available: either the sickness factors may be calculated on the basis of the adjusted sickness rates, or the valuation may be made on the "ages passed through" method, for a description of which the reader is referred to Watson's *Lectures on Friendly Society Finance*, pp. 68–74.

If it should appear from the investigation of the past experience that rates of sickness vary substantially according to the scales of benefit, or in other well-defined groups, it may be desirable to divide the data into groups corresponding thereto in order to give effect to the heterogeneity.

3. The standard sickness rates in general use are those known as the Manchester Unity 1893–97 Experience (A. W. Watson's tables), in which are included the rates for all the periods of sick pay usually met with. Occasionally, however, one finds unusual periods such as first 20 weeks, second 20 weeks and after 40 weeks, and in such a case it is necessary to construct rates. This can be done for ages up to 70 by interpolating between the rates for quinquennial ages given on p. 593 of the *Report for* 1912–13 *on the Administration of the National Insurance Act, Part 1*, whilst for ages over 70 it will probably be sufficient to take the first 20 weeks as equal to the first 13 weeks together with two-thirds of the second 13 weeks. An alternative method is to interpolate for each age between the tabulated functions, namely, first 3 months, second 3 months, second 6 months and second 12 months, for the actual period required.

The process of interpolation should be selected according to the circumstances of the case, and it is desirable, in any event, to test the effect of the interpolation by using the interpolated rates in calculating expected sickness claims for each period of sickness during the past inter-valuation period, and comparing the results with the actual experience.

4. The sickness values are obtained on working sheets arranged as follows:

Column (1) Age x.	Column (5) $K_x = \Sigma\,(4)$.
„ (2) $\overline{D}_x$.	„ (6) D_x.
„ (3) z_x.	„ (7) $\dfrac{K_x}{D_x}$.
„ (4) $H_x = (2) \times (3)$.	„ (8) $\Delta\,(7)$.*

A separate factor is required for each period for which a different rate of benefit is payable. When benefits and contributions are payable only to a fixed age, the factor is derived by summing the appropriate column, beginning with the value for the age one less than that at which the benefit ceases.

A good check upon the accuracy of the sickness factors is obtained by working out the factor for "all sickness", which should be equal

* Column (8) is employed for check purposes.

to the sum of the factors for the separate periods into which the total sickness is divided.

When contributions are not payable during sickness, a special factor equal to $\dfrac{1}{52 \cdot 18} \times$ (value of 1 per week during all periods of sickness) is required to value the loss on this account. If, however, it has been decided to add different loadings to the values of sick pay for the various periods, it will be necessary to separate this factor into its several parts in order that adjustments corresponding to the loadings may be made to the value of the loss of contributions.

5. Two methods are available for valuing the benefit payable on the death of a member's wife. Either the number of members who have actually received a wife's benefit may be ascertained and the remainder of the members, including bachelors, may be regarded as being entitled to a wife's death benefit, or the valuation may be made on the basis of the entire membership and a rate of claim may be incorporated in the valuation factor. In the first method it is usual to regard the wife's age as being the same as the member's, and to treat bachelors as if they were married, both of which assumptions slightly overestimate the liability, and the factor employed is A^1_{xx}. In the second method, a rate of claim (k_x) is derived from the society's experience by dividing the number of claims by the total membership of the society age by age, and roughly graduating the results. The factor is then simply $\dfrac{\Sigma(k_x \overline{D}_x)}{D_x}$. The suitability of the rates of claim should be tested from time to time, a test being particularly necessary when a change to lighter rates of mortality is being made in the valuation. If the society's mortality experience has become lighter, the rates of claim will have become lower and an omission to adjust the rates of claim when the lighter rates of mortality are introduced would have the anomalous effect of increasing the liability, since k_x, the variable annuity valued, would remain unchanged. In general, the first method is to be preferred.

Occasionally, instances are met with in which the rules provide for the payment, on the death of a member, of a fixed levy upon all the survivors. In these cases it is appropriate to include the value of the levy in the valuation balance sheet. The value may be obtained by the use of the formula $\dfrac{m\,(m-1)}{2}\,\bar{A}_{xx}$, where m is the number of members and x is an average age (see *Text-Book*, Part II, by G. King, p. 357). The age x may be found by means of the formula $m\mu_x = (a\mu_y + b\mu_z + \text{etc.})$, where a, b, etc. are the numbers of members aged y, z, etc.

6. The actual work of valuation, once the task of preparing the data has been performed, is comparatively simple. A convenient arrangement for the working sheet is the following:

Column (1)   Valuation age.
   ,,   (2)   No. of members.
   ,,   (3)   Column (2) in quinquennial groups.
   ,,   (4)   No. of shillings full sick pay.
   ,,   (5)   Column (4) in quinquennial groups.
   ,,   (6)   Value of sick pay of 1s. per week. Period.......
   ,,   (7)   Value of sick pay. Period....... (4) × (6).
   ,,   (8)
   ,,   (9) (4) × (8) | Factors and values of sick pay for other
   ,,   (10)   periods (at full rate, subsequently ad-
   ,,   (11) (4) × (10) | justed).
   ,,   (12)   Amount assured at death of members.
   ,,   (13)   Column (12) in quinquennial groups.
   ,,   (14) $\bar{A}_x$.
   ,,   (15)   Value of members' death benefit, (12) × (14).
   ,,   (16)   Amount of wives' death benefit.
   ,,   (17) $\bar{A}^1_{xx}$.
   ,,   (18)   Value of wives' death benefit, (16) × (17).
   ,,   (19)   No. of shillings per week of deferred annuity.
   ,,   (20)   Column (19) in quinquennial groups.
   ,,   (21) $\dfrac{52 \cdot 18}{20} \times {}_{M-x|}\bar{a}_x$ (M being the age at which annuities commence).
   ,,   (22)   Value of deferred annuity, (19) × (21).
   ,,   (23)   No. of shillings immediate annuity per week.
   ,,   (24)   Column (23) in quinquennial groups.

Column (25) $\dfrac{52\cdot18}{20}\times\bar{a}_x.$

„   (26) Value of immediate annuity, $(23)\times(25)$.

„   (27) Total benefit contributions per annum.

„   (28) $\bar{a}_x$ or $\bar{a}_{x:\overline{M-x}|}$ (if contributions cease at age M).

„   (29) Value of contributions, $(27)\times(28)$.

„   (30) Total value of benefits.

„   (31) Negative values.

In practice the work would have to be spread over several sheets, and it is an advantage to divide after column (11) and insert an additional column at the end showing the total value of sickness benefits age by age, after adjustment for the different rates of pay in the various periods and for any percentage loadings which it may have been decided to apply. The casts of the various data columns in groups of five ages are required for insertion on form F 40.

7. In section IV of form F 40 the question "What steps have been taken to ensure the elimination of negative values?" is asked, and although the instructions issued to public valuers no longer direct that no contract shall be treated as an asset, it seems to be implied that negative values should be eliminated. In the case of valuations made in accordance with the Industrial Assurance Act, 1923, it is definitely laid down in section 18 of the Act that the basis of valuation shall be such as to secure that no policy is treated as an asset. In any event negative values should always be eliminated; the dangers of not doing so are quite obvious. In order to be sure that all negative values were eliminated it would be necessary to make a valuation according to each age or group of ages at entry for which a different contribution was payable, but such a laborious procedure in the case of ordinary friendly societies is not as a rule deemed to be necessary. An inspection of the two columns (29), value of contributions, and (30), total value of benefits, will show the amount of negative values present on an aggregate valuation. The amount thus revealed will not be the total of negative values if within the data for any particular valuation age group there are entrants at different rates of contribution, as a positive reserve shown by the aggregate valuation may in fact be

the result of the addition of a larger positive reserve and a negative value. An investigation should be made to ascertain the appropriate addition to cover negative values thus hidden.

8. *Value of Assets.* If a certificate is not separately furnished or appended to the accounts giving the market value of the Stock Exchange securities, these should be valued by the actuary; and, where depreciation exists and has not been allowed for otherwise, a suitable reserve should be set up. If the society has investments in the form of land or buildings or other assets the value of which the actuary is himself unable to assess, he should ask for a report on their value, or, if the society does not wish to go to the expense of having a valuation made, for a certificate signed by the trustees stating the present realizable value. A certificate should also be furnished giving information regarding the mortgages, in particular as to whether they are fully secured and whether interest is regularly paid. The questions in section III of form F 40 relating to value of assets are asked in a very direct form, and the actuary must obviously ask in turn for full and duly authenticated information.

9. *Expenses of Management.* In the case of ordinary societies which are concerned mainly with granting sickness benefits, as distinct from collecting friendly societies, the expenses of management are usually met by means of separate contributions and other miscellaneous sources of income such as donations, fines, levies, etc., which are carried tp a separate fund. Provided the income of the management fund has been sufficient to meet the expenses no account is taken in the valuation of the transactions of this fund. The rules frequently provide for a special levy to be made in the event of a deficiency in the management fund, but societies are often loath to enforce the rule. The actuary will have to determine whether there are sufficient reasons for regarding as a good asset a deficiency in the management fund. If it appears that there is little likelihood of removing the deficit, a reserve should be set up in the valuation balance sheet.

10. Members of collecting friendly societies usually pay an inclusive contribution, a certain proportion of which is authorized by the rules to be transferred to the management fund. Often the rules also contain provision for the transfer to the management fund of a proportion, not exceeding a certain maximum percentage, of any surplus disclosed by a valuation, and collecting friendly societies frequently find it essential to adopt this method of meeting the expenses of management not covered by the proportion of the contributions allowed by the rules.

The 1923 Act (section 18 (1) (b)) prescribes that the basis of valuation shall be such as to place a proper value upon the liabilities, regard being had, amongst other things, to the expenses of management (including commission), and two courses are open to the actuary in a case where the society's expenses exceed the income from the authorized proportion of the contributions. He may make his valuation on the basis of taking credit for the full proportion of the contributions applicable under the rules to the benefits and state that his valuation is based on the assumption that if surpluses fail to materialize, and part of the income of the management fund is thus lost, the society will reduce its expenses of management. Some societies arrange that their expenses of management shall be automatically reduced if declared profits fall, and this is accomplished by fixing the remuneration of the staff partly on a fixed basis and partly on a profit-sharing basis. Alternatively, the actuary may include as a special reserve, inserted in the valuation balance sheet as an additional liability, a proportion of the present value of future contributions, the proportion being the difference between the percentage of the contributions absorbed in the actual expenses and the percentage allowed by the rules. The latter method is much to be preferred, and although it is not always practicable at once to reserve for the full difference, every opportunity should be taken of increasing the amount of the special reserve until the full provision is reached.

11. The valuation balance sheet will naturally follow the official form F 40, section V. In addition to the usual checking of all calculations it is advisable to scrutinize carefully the result, employing, wherever possible, overhead checks quite independent of the calculated results. Such checks will often enable the actuary to detect an error or omission—the latter being the more fruitful

source of trouble—which may have been made. An additional check on the general accuracy of the valuation can be obtained by drawing up a profit and loss account for the inter-valuation period. It is not suggested that it will show up a minor error, but it should ensure that no error of any magnitude has been made. Although form F 40 no longer contains the question formerly inserted, "To what causes may be attributed the surplus or deficiency shown by the valuation?" it is desirable that the actuary should give in section VI of the form, headed "Comments and Recommendations", an indication of the profits and losses realized by the society during the inter-valuation period, and how they have arisen.

12. In the analysis of the surplus the following items, excluding surplus carried forward from the preceding valuation, are among the most important to be considered:

(i) Interest earnings.
(ii) Sickness experience.
(iii) Mortality experience.
(iv) Withdrawal experience.
(v) Experience in regard to benefits other than sickness, annuity or death benefits.
(vi) Alterations of rules.
(vii) Changes in the valuation basis.
(viii) Realization of negative values.
(ix) Profit and loss from sale of investments.
(x) Appreciation or depreciation.
(xi) Admission of new members.
(xii) Special income or expenditure.

These items form the subject of the comments in the following paragraphs, which have been numbered to correspond with the list given above. It would often be a matter of considerable difficulty to analyse accurately the profit according to the sources from which it is derived, but great accuracy will rarely, if ever, be required.

(i) *Interest earnings.* The interest profit is the difference between the actual interest received and the "expected" interest. The latter may be taken with sufficient accuracy as simple interest at the valuation rate on the mean of the reserves held at the beginning and the end of the inter-valuation period, which, in the following notes, will be assumed to be five years. This method almost invariably overestimates slightly the "expected" interest, and if it is desired to obtain a closer approximation, a simple adjustment, which will usually be adequate, is to multiply the expected interest so obtained by the factor $(1 - \frac{1}{2}i)$, where i is the valuation rate of interest. It can be demonstrated algebraically that this adjustment will give a close approximation. A small practical point may be mentioned: care must be taken to see that in ascertaining the amount of interest actually received only that credited to the benefit fund is taken into account.

If a change has been made in the valuation basis, it will be necessary to make a valuation on the old basis in order to obtain the correct mean reserve upon which to calculate the amount of interest required by the valuation basis. Similarly, if a change of benefits has taken place during the quinquennium, it is convenient to make a valuation on the basis of the old benefits, using the reserve so obtained in order to obtain the mean reserve. It will be necessary to adjust the "expected" amount of interest so obtained on account of the difference between the amounts expected to be paid in benefits on the two bases and this adjustment may be taken as equal to interest at the valuation rate on the amount of the difference for one-half of the period between the date of operation of the change of benefits and the valuation date. A rough estimate of the adjustment is all that is required.

(ii) *Sickness experience.* The cash saving or loss due to the sickness experience can be readily ascertained from the examination previously made of the society's experience. It will usually be sufficient to convert the equivalent weeks into cash by reference to the average amount assured, but, if a more accurate estimate is desired, the experience at the different rates of full pay may be separately examined or the experience may be based on shillings of full pay. It is only necessary to remind readers that allowance must be made in calculating the "expected" for any loadings added to the sickness values.

(iii) *Mortality experience.* In the case of contracts comprising both sickness benefits (or annuity benefits) and death benefits, the net financial effect of variations in the mortality experience from the valuation standard will be the result of combining a profit and a loss. If the mortality has been light, a profit will have arisen on account of the death benefit whilst a loss will have been sustained on account of the sickness portion of the contract, the reverse being, of course, the case if the mortality experience has been a heavy one. The loss on account of the sickness benefit will be the reserves for that benefit which have to be held in respect of the additional number of survivors and will usually be greater than the profit arising from the death benefit.

Usually a composite contribution is payable in respect of the combined benefits and the matter therefore resolves itself, provided there is no question of a re-assurance of the death benefit, simply into whether the reserve held in respect of the whole contract is greater or less than the amount of the death benefit. If the reserve is greater, as it usually will be in the case of sickness benefit throughout life, a light mortality experience results in a loss on the valuation estimates, whilst if the reserve is less than the death benefit, as it may well be at the younger ages, or even at the higher ages when the sickness benefits terminate at the fixed age of 65 or 70, or if the amount of the death benefit is unusually large in comparison with the sickness benefit, a profit on the estimates will be secured. Where, however, the death benefit is re-assured with a central fund, as is usually the case with branches of the affiliated orders, other considerations arise and a discussion of the effect of variations in the mortality experience on the profit and loss account in these cases will be found in the next chapter.

(iv) *Withdrawal experience*. Where no benefit is payable on withdrawal—and it is only very rarely that a payment is made—the profit resulting from lapses in excess of the expected number is the full reserve held. If a benefit is payable, the profit is the difference between the expected and the actual strain. Provided that a rate of withdrawal is not incorporated in the valuation basis, all lapses, except those which occur at the ages where negative values arise, constitute a source of profit, the amount of the profit being the full reserve or the full reserve less the amount paid as a benefit, as the case may be. A loss on account of the withdrawal

5-2

experience would arise if rates of withdrawal which were too high had been included in the basis, but, as extreme caution is always exercised in fixing the rates of withdrawal, such a contingency should scarcely ever arise.

(v) *Benefits*, other than sickness, annuity and death benefits, are usually valued on a cost basis, and a comparison of the actual payments and the provision made in the valuation shows the amount of profit or loss.

(vi) *Alterations of rules.* The effect of an alteration of rule is best analysed into (1) the profit or loss which would have arisen if the change had been made at the valuation date, and (2) the profit or loss due to the difference between the conditions of the new and the old rules arising from the operation of the new rules during the period between their registration and the valuation date. The first item is directly ascertained by making a valuation on the basis of the old rules and taking the difference between the reserves on that valuation and the official valuation. The second item may be found by accumulating with interest at the valuation rate the difference between the balances of "expected" income over "expected" expenditure on the basis of the old and new rules. The result is the amount by which the fund should have been greater or less, on the basis of the valuation, had the new rules not been in operation before the valuation date, and is therefore the loss or profit due to the operation of the new rules to that date.

(vii) *Changes in the valuation basis.* The effect of a change in the valuation basis is determined by making a valuation on the old basis. It should be added that, in the case of small societies, short methods may legitimately be adopted for the valuation on the old basis, e.g. a valuation by means of an average age, or by groups of ages, as the result will be sufficiently accurate for this purpose.

(viii) *Realization of negative values.* The calculation of the amount of profit which has arisen from this source, if performed accurately, would entail an examination of all contracts which, at any time during the quinquennium, were within the range of negative value ages and the investigation would have to be made according to ages at entry. Usually, however, the amount of the profit does not justify more than the labour involved in deriving an estimate on the aggregate basis, but cases are met with, generally where a flat rate of contribution is payable over a long range of ages at entry, when the profit from this source is very considerable. In the case of a contract which had a negative value at the last valuation and still has a negative value at the present valuation, the profit, as no reserve has been held, consists of the contributions which have been paid during the quinquennium, less the "expected" cost of benefits, whilst if, during the course of the quinquennium, the contract has changed from a negative value to a positive value, it is necessary to deduct also from the contributions paid the amount of the reserves now held.

(ix) *Profit and loss from sale of investments*. This item is readily determined from the accounts.

In regard to National Savings Certificates the difference between the amounts at which they stood in the accounts and the amounts obtained when they are surrendered should be regarded as interest and not as profit on sale of investments. It is advisable to write up the value of these certificates each year and to take credit in the accounts for the accrued interest.

(x) *Appreciation or depreciation*. Some societies make a practice of having their assets valued at the end of each financial year and write the book values up or down to the market prices. In these cases there should be a corresponding entry in the revenue account showing the amounts added or written off. Account must also be taken of any differences between the amounts, if any, which have been set up as reserves for depreciation in the last and in the present valuation balance sheets.

(xi) *Admission of new members*. It not infrequently happens, owing to the valuation basis being more stringent than that on which the rates of contribution were originally calculated, that a positive reserve at date of entry is required in respect of each new entrant, and, if a large number have been admitted during the five years, a considerable strain may have been imposed. In section II of form F 40 details are asked of the values, for six specified ages at entry, of the contributions and of the benefits on the basis adopted for the valuation, and these values will show at once whether the strain is appreciable or not. The calculation of the actual amount is a simple matter.

(xii) *Special income or expenditure.* Friendly societies sometimes receive donations and legacies, and, although these are usually appropriated to the management fund, which, in the case of some of the older county and local societies, has by these means reached a considerable sum, they are sometimes added to the benefit fund.

In schemes of appropriation, in which surplus is allotted in shares to the members, the shares of members who secede are frequently re-transferred to the benefit fund. These and other items not taken into account in the valuation constitute a profit, and any expenditure not allowed for in the valuation basis must be treated as a loss.

CHAPTER VIII

DISTRICT FUNERAL FUNDS AND SPECIAL SICKNESS BENEFITS

1. Reference has already been made in a previous chapter to the position of the districts in the constitution of the affiliated orders, and one of the functions of the district is the administration of the district funeral fund with which the lodge death benefits are re-assured. The liability for the payment of funeral benefits usually represents a comparatively small part of the total liabilities undertaken by a lodge, and, in the early days of the friendly society movement, the desirability of re-assuring the death benefits probably assumed an exaggerated importance. As Watson points out in his *Lectures*, the real need is re-assurance against abnormal survivorship. Variations in the experienced rates of mortality affect in opposite directions the cost of sickness benefit and the cost of death benefit, and a scheme of re-assurance which deals only with the death benefit may favour some of the lodges at the expense of the others. As is explained in Chapter VII, a light mortality experience almost invariably results in increased sickness reserves and ultimately in increased sickness payments, and a society which is itself liable for the payment of both sickness and funeral benefit is able to set off the small saving on the latter against the loss on the former. When the death benefit is re-assured with a central funeral fund and the mortality experience of each individual lodge over a long period reflects the mortality experience of the district as a whole, the re-assurance arrangement will be mutually advantageous, but a lodge whose mortality experience is consistently lighter than that of the district as a whole suffers a double loss, firstly, on accoun of the increased strain in respect of the cost of sickness benefits, and, secondly, because it pays more than its strictly equitable share of the actual cost of death benefits. On the other hand a lodge which experiences rates of mortality consistently heavier than those of the district as a whole secures a double advantage.

2. District funeral funds may be divided into two main classes:

    (i) those which operate on a levy basis and which have no accumulated fund;

and (ii) those which are based on a contribution method, and which involve the accumulation of capital.

In the Manchester Unity the levy type is that now most frequently in operation, whilst in the Ancient Order of Foresters the contribution method is more usual.

3. Watson describes in his *Lectures* the levy methods adopted in the past by districts of the Manchester Unity, many of which worked inequitably between the lodges, but at the present time the great majority of non-accumulative funeral funds are supported by what is known as the equitable levy method. The expected claims for the year of each lodge and the whole district are estimated by reference to the amount at risk at the beginning of the year and the appropriate rate of mortality age by age, and the actual claims for the year are then divided amongst the lodges in proportion to these expected claims. It has been found possible in practice, without any great loss of accuracy, to group the amount at risk in age groups, with a very considerable reduction in the work involved.

4. The accumulative funeral funds are supported by the payment of fixed contributions which may be in the form of:

    (*a*) a contribution graduated according to age at entry,

or (*b*) a fixed proportion of the total benefit contributions received by the lodge.

Alternative (*b*) provides a very convenient and usually sufficiently accurate method, provided the benefits and contributions are payable throughout life, the underlying assumption being that for all ages at entry the cost of the funeral benefit is approximately a constant proportion of the cost of the total benefit. When, however, as is now frequently the case, sickness benefits and contributions cease at, say, age 65 or 70, and the funeral benefit is payable whenever death may occur, this assumption is no longer even approximately correct and this method cannot be employed.

The contributions are either paid over to the district funeral fund to accumulate in the hands of the district or paid into a separate lodge fund and held in trust by the lodge for the district funeral fund. If the latter method is followed, the district merely calls up or levies from the lodges enough to meet current claims, the basis of demand being usually a proportion of the amount held in trust. In the case of many such funds, the capital held in trust is by rule credited with interest at only 3 per cent. per annum, a rate which, whilst probably not inappropriate in earlier days, is now much below the rate earned upon the lodge funds as a whole. The balance of the interest revenue is credited to the lodge funds, and, if the capital held in trust by lodges actually represented in individual cases the liability for funeral benefits, no inequity would result. After the fund has been in operation for a number of years, however, the amounts held in trust may differ widely from the reserves in respect of the funeral liabilities of individual lodges, with the result that the lodges with disproportionately large amounts of capital held in trust secure more than their equitable share of the interest earned in excess of 3 per cent. upon the money held on behalf of the funeral fund. This inequity is not inherent in the scheme of re-assurance and could be, and in many cases is being, remedied as regards the future, by an alteration of rule increasing the rate of interest to be credited upon the capital held in trust.

5. It frequently happens that the district funeral fund valuation is made at a rate of interest different from that employed in the valuation of the lodge, and it is consequently necessary for the funeral liabilities to be valued at two rates of interest. The surplus or deficiency disclosed by the district funeral fund valuation is apportioned amongst the lodges, and the share of each lodge appears in its valuation balance sheet as a credit or debit item.

Surpluses in district funeral funds arise usually from three main sources, namely, light mortality, secessions, and excess interest, the latter being by far the most important, whilst deficiencies are generally due to the essential inadequacy of the contributions. The surplus or deficiency should be apportioned amongst the lodges by a method which has regard to the actual sources of profit or loss, but there is no necessity to adopt an elaborate method of division. Profit from interest could be divided in proportion to reserves, profit from mortality in accordance with the death strain and other profits according to contribution income.

6. The effect upon the financial position of a lodge of re-assuring its funeral benefits with a central fund is very fully dealt with in Watson's *Lectures*, pp. 82–84, to which the student is referred, and only a brief reference to this matter is made here.

Under the levy system the profit or loss arising from the mortality experience should be ascertained, in the first place, as if the lodge were itself responsible for the funeral liabilities. A further item of profit (or loss) then arises if the amount paid in levies to the district funeral fund by the lodge is less (or greater) than the amount of funeral claims refunded. This item includes any profit or loss due to a defective system of re-assurance, and for further information on this point the student is referred to Watson's *Lectures*. Where, however, the equitable levy system is in operation no profit or loss arises from defects in the method of levying, and the profit or loss ascertained in this manner represents the true profit or loss, on the basis of valuation, due to the actual mortality experience.

If an accumulative district funeral fund is in operation, the profit or loss account of the lodge should be prepared by ignoring entirely both the funeral benefits and the corresponding contributions. If, for instance, a light mortality experience had operated during the inter-valuation period, the resulting loss would be ascertained by reference to the deficit in the number of actual deaths in each age group and the average reserve for sickness and other benefits not re-assured. It is desirable, perhaps, to remind the student that the share of the district funeral fund surplus (or deficiency) allocated to the lodge constitutes an additional item of profit (or loss).

7. The following paragraphs deal with the valuation of special types of sickness benefit.

A type of benefit not infrequently met with is full sick pay for, say, 26 weeks and half-pay for a further 26 weeks, no further sickness benefit being allowed until a certificate of recovery has been furnished. The usual "off period" regulations apply to benefit during the first and second 6 months, and as it is not possible, when sick pay has been received for 52 consecutive weeks or assumed consecutive weeks, to claim further benefit in respect of the same illness, the conditions governing the receipt of benefit are the same as those obtaining in the Manchester Unity sickness experience, except that no "after 12 months" benefit is payable. In such a case the benefits can be valued by the usual first and second 6 months factors, no continuous sickness benefit being valued.

8. More frequently, however, where the rules of a society do not specifically provide for continuous sick pay, members are merely required to be off the funds for a stipulated period, say 12 months, after having received full pay for 26 weeks and half-pay for a further 26 weeks. In such circumstances it would not be correct to value the benefits by employing only the first and second 6 months sickness factors, since, as no certificate of recovery is required, a member could claim a further cycle of full and half-benefits in respect of the same illness by merely complying with the conditions requiring him to be off the funds for the specified period. The conditions governing the receipt of full and half-pay in such cases are clearly not comparable with those of the standard experience, and if a proper value is to be placed upon this benefit some allowance must be made for claims after the first 12 months, as the Manchester Unity Experience does not provide for more than one cycle of full and half-benefit in respect of the same illness. The sickness benefit under such conditions becomes full pay for 26 weeks, half-pay for 26 weeks, nil for 52 weeks, full pay for 26 weeks and so on. A suitable basis for valuation of such a benefit is, as described by Watson in his *Lectures*, p. 17, full pay for 26 weeks, half-pay for 26 weeks and three-eighths of full pay after 78 weeks. The importance of ascertaining precisely which of the two types of benefit is in operation will be appreciated in view of the difference in liability exhibited by the two methods of valuation.

9. An exceptional type of benefit, which has been met with, is full pay in all sickness until the member has drawn an amount equal to the total contributions paid, followed by a reduced rate of benefit. One method of valuation is to ascertain by reference to a suitable standard table the age at which a member will have received the limit of full sick pay on the assumption that his actual claims will be in future exactly in accordance with the standard table, and to value the full pay as ceasing at that age, using the "all-sickness" rates. The age at which full pay is deemed to cease should be re-calculated at successive valuations in order to allow for any deviation of the actual claims to date from the standard rates. It would probably be sufficiently accurate for practical purposes to take this age as the nearest quinquennial age, whilst, if the society were fairly large, an average age at which full pay is assumed to cease could be calculated for each attained age by reference to the aggregate sick pay already drawn by members included in the group.

An alternative method, which could be applied in the case of a large and old-established society, would be to construct rates of sickness deduced from the society's own experience during a normal period and to employ the ordinary method of valuation. It would be desirable to investigate separately the experience of members in grouped ages at entry in order to discover whether any difference in the experience was sufficiently pronounced to necessitate the valuation's being made in groups according to age at entry. The future sickness claims under this scheme of benefits will be influenced by the claims already made, a feature which is not characteristic of the claims under the ordinary type of sickness benefit, and it would therefore be particularly necessary to examine the trend of the experience over a fairly long period, in order to ascertain whether the rates of sickness now experienced at the higher ages would be likely to apply to the members who are now at the middle ages, when they in their turn reached the older ages. This feature seems to lay the method of valuation open to criticism. In view of the possibility of having to make frequent alterations in the assumed rates of sickness, some advantage would perhaps be gained by the adoption of R. P. Hardy's "ages passed through" method of valuation.

A somewhat similar problem arises in cases in which a limit is set to the total amount to be drawn by any member in sickness benefit. Methods of valuation similar to those mentioned in the preceding paragraphs could be employed, but the same criticism applies in connection with the second method.

10. As an example of the diversity of types of sickness benefit, it may be interesting to mention that of a fairly large county society which granted full pay for 52 weeks and reduced pay thereafter during the first 35 years of membership and full benefit in all sickness after the completion of 35 years of membership. The benefit can be valued as full pay throughout, the reduction after 52 weeks during the first 35 years of membership being valued as a temporary (negative) benefit ceasing at an age depending upon the age at entry. Such a system of benefit has little to recommend it, since it is in the early years, when his responsibilities are heavy, that a member requires the maximum insurance. Moreover, from a financial point of view the system is open to serious objection in that it is almost certain to lead to a heavy excess in the cost of claims at the older ages. In the case of the particular society in which it was in operation, it has now been abandoned in favour of the more usual system.

11. *Unemployment Benefit.* As has been previously mentioned, societies granting this type of benefit almost invariably limit their membership to employees in a particular trade. Quite frequently the employers make donations to the funds and are therefore interested in the financial side of the society. The facilities for securing employment are usually much wider than is the case amongst the general population, and in fact one of the functions of such a society is to secure employment for its members. As a consequence the statistics relating to unemployment, derived from the national records, afford little guidance as to the probable experience of these societies.

The valuation of the unemployment benefit is usually made by reference to a rate of claim based upon the experience of one of the large societies, suitable adjustments being made when necessary. It will be appreciated that the officials of the society have much less control over the unemployment claims than over the sickness claims, and the former are in fact much less susceptible of precise measurement. The valuation basis should be strong enough to allow for the wider fluctuations in the experience.

CHAPTER IX

THE VALUATION REPORT

1. In submitting the results of his valuation, the actuary is required to complete the official form F 40, the last section of which, entitled "Comments and Recommendations", usually takes the form of a report. It is often found to be more convenient to deal in the report with some of the questions in the earlier section of the form, the answer to the question consisting simply of a reference to the appropriate section of the report.

The report is usually addressed to the committee of management of the society, and it is well to bear in mind that, although a report on a valuation must contain technical references, it should be couched in language which may be readily understood by those to whom it is addressed. Although, in the case of larger societies, the members of the committee of management have often had considerable experience of problems connected with actuarial valuations and readily appreciate the points which the actuary wishes to make, those responsible for the administration of smaller societies are often able to devote only a limited amount of time to the society's affairs and are more likely to carry out his recommendations if these are clearly stated in non-technical language. It should be remembered that the actuary is the person best qualified to advise the society on financial matters, and the opportunity should be taken in the report of suggesting any practical measures for improving the society's methods or organization.

The following is a convenient scheme for the report.

(a) Introduction

2. It is usual to open the report with a statement giving the number of members and the amount of funds and a comparison of the present figures with those of the preceding valuation. Other statistics of a general character likely to be of interest to the members may also be included here.

(b) General Observations

3. Mention should be made of any peculiar features in the rules which may have a bearing on the valuation. In cases where, for technical reasons, it is necessary to disregard the operation of a particular rule, the circumstances should be explained and the assumptions made should be fully stated. The attention of the members is thus at once drawn to what may be a fundamental condition of the valuation, and the position of the actuary is safeguarded. Under this heading should be mentioned any alterations of rule which may have taken place since the last valuation. It is also convenient to include here any observation which may arise out of the answers to section II of form F 40 regarding the contribution income.

It is sometimes found that the practice of a society is not in accordance with its registered rules, and the actuary should state whether the valuation is based on the existing practice or on the registered rules. The answer to question II (c) of form F 40 can then take the form of a reference to the report.

(c) Experience

4. An important section from the point of view of the officers of the society is the result of the investigation of the society's experience during the inter-valuation period, and it is here that it is often possible to assist the management by pointing out the directions in which the society should endeavour to improve its experience.

5. The sickness experience may be exhibited either in the form of a comparison of the actual weeks of sickness benefit with the expected weeks, or in the form of a financial statement showing the expected and the actual cost. In the case of large societies both methods are usually adopted, whilst for small societies the financial comparison in the manner required by section IV (d) of form F 40 will usually be sufficient. The experience can conveniently be shown in the following form:

Age group	First period			Second period, etc.	All periods
	Actual weeks	Expected weeks	Percentage of actual to expected		
Quinquennial age groups All ages					

From such a table it can be seen at once which period is responsible for any excess of sickness which the society may be experiencing, and which rate of benefit should be operated on if the position should be so serious as to call for a reduction in benefits. A scrutiny of the experience of the separate age groups will show whether an excess arises in a particular age group, or whether it is in general the younger or the older members who are responsible. Such information should be of assistance to the management in indicating the direction in which to attempt to secure an improvement in the experience by the adoption of stricter methods of administration.

6. It is often useful to include also a statement in which the actual and expected weeks of sickness are reduced to equivalent weeks of full pay, details being given in age groups. In cases where several rates of sick pay are in operation, a corresponding statement expressed in terms of cost of sick pay may be included, as such a statement shows in a very direct manner the financial effect of the experience and is often more helpful in bringing out its significance than the statement based on weeks of sickness. In the case of smaller societies this information is only given in total, but indications of any special features of the experience should be noted. For a full discussion of the subject the reader is referred to Watson's paper "The Analysis of a Sickness Experience" (*J.I.A.* Vol. LXII, p. 12).

A description of the loadings, if any, added to the sickness values should be included under this heading, together with the reasons for their inclusion.

7. The comments on the mortality experience must of necessity be mainly of a technical character, and possibly the only statements of interest to the society will be the remarks on any change of basis which may have been made in the valuation and the effect of the change, or on the probability of a change becoming necessary at a future valuation. The fact that, contrary to what the ordinary member might expect to be the case, a light mortality experience is usually a financially unfavourable feature, may be mentioned with advantage, if the comment is appropriate.

8. In cases where rates of withdrawal are incorporated in the basis, it is as well to give a statement of the number of expected and actual withdrawals in age groups.

(d) RATE OF INTEREST AND INVESTMENT OF FUNDS

9. A useful service can often be rendered to the society by drawing attention to the manner in which its assets are invested. It is as well to bear in mind that, apart from their connection with friendly societies, many of those responsible for the management, especially of the smaller societies, have little experience of problems of investment, and that they will often welcome expert advice in order that they may make the most of the advantages which the current conditions offer. Although the funds of friendly societies are in general very well invested, cases are still sometimes met with where unremunerative investments are retained, and even where substantial sums, far more than sufficient to cover current needs, are left on deposit at the bank or in the Post Office; in these cases the importance of securing a good rate of interest should be stressed. The rate of interest employed should be mentioned and, where no action has been taken in regard to the other elements of the valuation basis on account of the existence of a substantial margin between the rate of interest earned and that assumed, the fact should be noted.

If it has been found necessary to set up a reserve for depreciation, the valuer should mention his reasons for so doing, and the amount of the reserve. If he has been unable to secure satisfactory evidence of the value of the assets, he should state the fact and add that the result of the valuation is only valid if the assets are of the value for which credit has been taken in the valuation balance sheet.

(e) Valuation Basis

10. Only a brief statement of the valuation basis should be necessary, as the main points in connection with it will have been already discussed in the paragraphs dealing with the experience. In cases where the rates employed have not been published, details must be furnished, and it is convenient to give them in an appendix. A description of the basis is required in section IV (c) of form F 40.

(f) Expenses of Management

11. The report should state what provision has been made to meet the future expenses of management. When a deficiency exists in the management fund attention should be drawn to it and, if no reserve has been made on account of it, the reasons should be given. Measures designed to remove the deficiency should be suggested, and these may take the form of imposing a levy, usually authorized by the rules, of increasing the contributions for management, or, where the society possesses a substantial surplus and the circumstances warrant it, of a transfer out of the surplus to the management fund.

(g) Result of the Valuation

12. In the course of the valuation an analysis of the surplus or deficiency will have been made, wherever practicable, and this furnishes the material for the comments on the result of the valuation. It is not, as a rule, necessary to give precise details of the actual amounts but the main results should be indicated. A valuable purpose is thereby served, as the officials and members are not only encouraged to continue their efforts to maintain sources of profit, but are reminded of any adverse features which have retarded the prosperity of the society.

(h) Recommendations

13. From the point of view of the members, the last section of the report is perhaps the most valuable. Where a serious deficiency exists and there are no sources of future profits (not already taken into account) which can be relied upon gradually to reduce the deficiency, remedial measures should be suggested. It should be borne in mind, however, that very drastic reductions in benefits or increases in contributions are unlikely to be accepted by the members and, even if accepted, are likely to defeat their object as they may well result in the secession of the younger members. It is preferable in these circumstances to remove the deficiency by stages over two or three quinquennia.

14. Whether a reduction of benefits or an increase of contributions should be suggested depends upon the circumstances. The following methods of operating on the sickness benefits are available:

(i) A reduction by a flat percentage in the amount of sick pay for all periods. Such a reduction would be appropriate when there was no marked excess at any particular rate of pay.

(ii) A reduction in the rate of sick pay for particular periods, whether one or more, according to the period or periods which showed a bad experience.

(iii) A reduction in the period of payment for full pay or reduced pay or both.

(iv) The substitution of a temporary benefit for the continuous benefit. In this case, claims at the lowest rate would be allowed continuously for a period of, say, 52 weeks only and a member who had received sick pay for the full period of 52 weeks would be required to remain off the funds for a considerable period, say two years, before being allowed to resume benefit; and even then he would only be allowed to revert to the lowest rate unless in the meantime he had recovered. Such a revision, however, is very drastic and should only be suggested in exceptional circumstances, but it might be appropriate in a case where it was found that the lowest rate of pay was being regarded as a pension or old age allowance.

(v) The introduction of a limit to the total amount which may be drawn in sick pay by each member, or where such a limit already exists, a reduction in the amount of the limit. These limits are, however, contrary to the spirit of insurance, and only in extreme cases should the introduction of a limit for the first time be advised.

(vi) An extension of the off period governing the return to full pay or to half-pay or both, with the object of controlling the cost of benefits.

(vii) A reduction of the age up to which sickness benefits are payable, as for example, from throughout life to age 70, or from age 70 (if benefits already cease at that age) to some earlier age, say 65. This method is, however, open to the grave objection that it must operate inequitably unless the older members receive some compensation in the form of another benefit, such as an endowment or an increase in the death benefit. Moreover, unless compensation were provided it is unlikely that such a reform would be adopted by a general meeting of the members, as it is not difficult to see that the older members, who would be deprived of their sickness benefits, would object strongly.

A disadvantage of increasing contributions is that it is liable to cause the younger members to leave the society, particularly if they are young enough to be able to secure a better contract with another society, and also, perhaps, to drive out those members who do not claim when ill. If, however, the contributions payable are low, an increase of contributions might be proposed in conjunction with a reduction in sickness benefits. Where the contributions are inadequate they ought certainly to be increased for new entrants.

Only in very exceptional circumstances should a reduction in the amount of the death benefit be suggested.

It should be borne in mind that a change in the scale of benefit or the conditions under which it is receivable may affect very materially the character of the experience, and for this reason it is not always necessary to reduce the benefit by as much as might appear to be required in order to secure solvency. Frequently better results are obtained if a moderate measure of reform, likely to secure the approval of the members, is suggested, to be followed, if necessary, by a further smaller revision after the next valuation. Watson deals fully with this aspect of the subject in pp. 84 *et seq.* of his *Lectures.*

15. When a surplus has been disclosed, a demand is usually made for an appropriation and schemes which are impracticable (and often inequitable) are not infrequently put forward by the members. Fortunately, however, the advice of the actuary is usually sought—many societies have in fact a rule which requires that the adoption of a scheme of appropriation shall be subject to the approval of the actuary. The objects to which appropriated surplus may be, and is frequently, applied are the following:

(i) Increase of present benefits or the introduction of new benefits.

(ii) Reduction of contributions.

(iii) Establishment of a reserve fund.

(iv) Transfer to a distress fund.

(v) Transfer to the management fund.

(vi) Transfer from branch to central fund.

(i) *Increase of benefits*

16. Increases in the amount of sick pay are usually very costly and should only be made with caution. It is not safe to assume that the cost of an increase will be in proportion to the present value of the existing benefits, as it is fairly usual to find that an increase in benefits results in an increase in the number and duration, of claims, the experience deteriorating as the rate of sickness benefit increases. If the society insists on increasing the sickness benefits in circumstances which do not secure the approval of the actuary it is best to suggest the setting aside of a separate fund from which the additional benefits may be paid as long as the fund lasts. Where the periods of full and reduced pay are short, especially in the case of those societies which have at some time reduced those periods owing to a deficiency, an extension of one or both of the periods is a form of increase of benefit which is less open to objection.

An increase in the death benefit, particularly where the amount of this benefit is small in relation to the sick pay and where sick pay continues throughout life, is a very good form of additional benefit.

Occasionally the members ask for a cash bonus, but such a distribution is to be deprecated as not being in harmony with the object for which the society was established. There is, however, no objection to the introduction of an endowment benefit payable when the member reaches the age of 65 or 70 years.

(ii) *Reduction of contributions*

17. A popular form of appropriation is that by which the members' contributions are reduced or entirely redeemed, either at once or after the attainment of the fixed age of 65 or 70, the reduction being calculated either for the members as a whole or individually. Not infrequently, a distribution of surplus takes the form of a division into shares according to the duration of membership. The shares so allotted are transferred to a separate appropriation fund and the member is allowed to draw on his share, whilst he has a balance available, (*a*) to provide additional sick pay at a small maximum weekly rate fixed by the society, (*b*) to provide an endowment at age 65 or 70, or (*c*) to pay contributions during sickness or when the member is in distressed circumstances, any balance remaining at the member's death being added to his funeral benefit. These conditions are sometimes further extended to allow the balance to be drawn upon to provide maternity benefits or to defray medical, optical and dental expenses, or the cost of convalescent home or hospital treatment. This form of distribution is well adapted to the needs of individual members and has much to recommend it. It is an advantage not to credit the appropriation fund with interest, as this not only ensures a higher yield for the benefit fund (thus safeguarding the latter fund and providing a source of profit for future surpluses), but also makes the book-keeping of this fund simpler inasmuch as no further allocation to individual accounts is ever necessary. The total of the individual balances is thus always equal to the fund, provided, as is usual, that the shares of the members who lapse are re-transferred to the benefit fund or some other fund.

(iii) *Reserve fund*

18. The whole of a disclosed surplus would not as a rule be certified as appropriable and an additional reserve would thus be retained. As an alternative, a portion of the surplus could be transferred to create a reserve or contingencies fund, to be used to make good any losses resulting from depreciation of securities or to meet other exceptional circumstances.

(iv) *Transfer to a distress fund*

19. Many societies establish a distress fund, and such a fund is capable of serving a very useful purpose. Disbursements from the fund are entirely at the discretion of the members, who are thus able to afford relief to distressed members quickly and without hampering restrictions. The establishment of these funds should be encouraged.

(v) *Transfer to the management fund*

20. It has already been mentioned that in most of the ordinary friendly societies a separate contribution for management is charged, and in many instances it has been found that, whilst the contribution charged before the War was adequate, the increased cost of salaries, printing, etc., has resulted in a deficiency in the management fund. As an alternative to increasing the contributions, societies frequently transfer amounts of surplus to this fund, and, since all members thereby secure an advantage, it is not an unreasonable course to adopt although, strictly speaking, it may be inequitable. Perhaps the principal objection is that the expenses of management may rise unduly when the members are not called upon directly to bear the additional cost.

(vi) *Transfer to a central fund*

21. Although some of the larger orders have for many years had central relief funds, they were only able to grant assistance to a very limited extent to branches which found themselves in difficulty, since the income of the relief funds, derived from a small contribution or levy per head of the membership of the order, was comparatively small. In 1921 the annual conference of the Manchester Unity Friendly Society inaugurated a scheme for affording assistance to branches in difficulty which has met with entire success, and the principle has since been adopted by at least one other large order. Under this scheme, all branches were required to transfer to the Unity Reserve Fund such proportion of their surpluses as should be determined by the annual conference, the proportion actually decided upon for three successive valuations being 25 per cent., 15 per cent., and 5 per cent., and the funds so raised were devoted to making it possible for lodges which had been compelled to reduce benefits or increase contributions to revert to their original schemes of benefits and contributions. All lodges were required to revert to their original tables, and those whose degree of solvency on a 4 per cent. valuation was less than 95 per cent. received a credit sufficient to raise the degree of solvency* to that level. During the years immediately following the War, friendly societies enjoyed a period of exceptional prosperity, due chiefly to the high rates of interest then prevailing and to the general light sickness experience, and the far-sighted policy of this society in taking advantage of the circumstances has been fully justified.

* In calculating the degree of solvency, which is only required when the valuation reveals a deficiency, the liabilities are taken as the present value of the benefits and the assets as the liabilities increased by the deficiency. The degree of solvency is the ratio of the assets (including the present value of future contributions) to the liabilities. This method of calculating the degree of solvency may yield a ratio very different from that which would result from a comparison of the assets (excluding the value of future contributions) and the net liability as these terms are understood in life assurance practice.

CHAPTER X

FRIENDLY SOCIETIES SINCE THE ADVENT OF NATIONAL HEALTH INSURANCE

1. A paper recently submitted to the Institute by Burrows under this title (see *J.I.A.* Vol. LXIII, p. 307) deals exhaustively with modern developments of friendly societies, and it is thought that a summary of this paper (consisting almost entirely of a series of extracts) would form a useful concluding chapter.

2. With the advent of National Health Insurance the friendly society movement in this country entered upon a new phase of its history. The period which has elapsed since 1911 has witnessed far-reaching changes affecting not only the methods by which friendly societies conduct their operations and the nature of the benefits they offer, but also the character of their experience and even the outlook of the members.

One of the immediate effects of the passing of the National Insurance Act, 1911, was to drive out of existence a number of the smaller and less capably managed friendly societies and to induce many others to join the larger affiliated orders, which thus received an appreciable addition to their membership, but since that date these orders have shown a tendency to decline in numbers. Although the affiliated orders and the majority of the societies of the "accumulative" type have experienced difficulty in maintaining their adult membership during the last twenty years, it is interesting to note that registered friendly societies as a whole have been able to add considerably to their aggregate membership, due largely to the growth of deposit societies.

FINANCIAL PROGRESS

3. Whilst the accumulative friendly societies have as a whole suffered a reduction in their membership since 1910, the improvement in their financial position has, however, been very considerable. At the valuations of societies without branches which fell due within

the period 1908–12 the average degree of solvency was 17s. 10d. in the £, whilst, at the valuations of societies in this group fifteen years later, the corresponding degree of solvency was 20s. 2d. in the £. The progress of the affiliated orders was even more remarkable.

INVESTMENT OF FUNDS

4. Those responsible for the management of friendly societies have in recent years paid much greater attention to the question of the remunerative investment of funds, and this has resulted in marked changes in the proportion of the funds placed in different types of investment. Deposits with the National Debt Commissioners, an item which used to appear fairly frequently in friendly society accounts, have now been reduced to very small proportions and investments in mortgages and land and buildings (including mortgages in possession), which used to represent the major part of the total funds, have diminished considerably, although they still constitute the most important class. Government securities have grown considerably in favour—due no doubt to the much higher rate of interest obtainable thereon and also to the patriotic motive which operated during the War. Municipal securities represent practically the same percentage of the total funds of friendly societies as in 1910, the increase in investments of this type in the case of the affiliated orders being offset by the reduction in the proportion of such investments by other societies. The more enterprising investment policy of friendly societies generally, coupled with the considerably increased rate of interest obtainable upon first-class securities during and since the War, has naturally led to a marked improvement in the rates of interest earned upon their funds and to a general rise in the rates of interest employed in valuations. This latter factor has contributed greatly to the improved financial position which their more recent valuations have disclosed, though it should be mentioned that the margins existing between the rates of interest earned and those employed in the valuations have for the most part increased appreciably since 1910, whilst, generally speaking, the strength of valuation bases has in other respects been more than maintained.

Financial Reforms

5. After friendly societies first became subject to periodical valuations it was for many years an all too frequent experience for deficiencies to be disclosed, despite the fact that the valuation bases were in many cases none too strong. It was a long time before the necessity for taking definite steps to remedy the financial positions revealed became generally recognized. For many years, the only means of dealing with deficiencies disclosed by valuations was for the members themselves to agree to reductions of benefit or increases of contributions or to both. In the case of independent societies these were, normally, the only possible courses open, but branches of the affiliated orders were in a more favourable position, as it was possible for them to inaugurate schemes under which the more prosperous branches afforded financial assistance to weaker branches. This assistance usually took the form of a single or periodical monetary grant, or, alternatively, the branch was relieved of the payment of the funeral benefits of its older members. The scheme introduced by the Manchester Unity has been mentioned in an earlier chapter, and for fuller details of this and of schemes adopted by other societies the student should refer to Burrows's paper.

Changes in Type of Benefit

6. Reference was made earlier in the chapter to a change of outlook which has taken place amongst the members of friendly societies in recent years. It has always been an article of faith amongst members of the accumulative friendly societies that—to employ a phrase culled from the initiation charge used in one of the affiliated orders—membership involved "more than a mere monetary contract". The introduction of State Insurance, however, immediately led to an accession to their ranks of a large number of members who regarded their membership mainly, if not solely, in the light of an insurance contract. The increasing emphasis upon the monetary contract aspect of friendly society membership and the growing aversion of the ordinary member from active participation in the affairs of his society have, not unnaturally, been accompanied by a tendency among accumulative societies to attach more and more importance to types of benefit in which the individual member secures far greater control over his personal contributions. It is, of course, the demand for this type of benefit which accounts for the remarkable growth of deposit and dividing societies. This in turn has led accumulative societies to adopt tables of benefit somewhat similar to those of deposit and dividing societies in order to attract new members. Curiously enough, contemporaneously with this effort of accumulative societies to borrow from the methods of deposit and dividing societies, these latter societies have returned the compliment by exhibiting a growing concern as to their actuarial soundness, and have shown an increasing desire to buttress their financial position by the building up of reserve funds.

7. A number of societies, particularly county societies, have for very many years past met the demand for the deposit society type of benefit by creating a separate deposit or Holloway section. More recently, however, a number of schemes have been adopted which involve no departure from actuarial principles. The main feature of these schemes is the addition to an ordinary sickness contract (providing, however, only for sickness benefits up to the age of 65 or 70) of a contribution which is accumulated at a fixed rate of interest so as to yield a lump sum payment on the attainment of the age of 65. In the event of death before that age the accumulated amount of the supplementary contributions is payable, sometimes with a guaranteed minimum, smaller sums being payable on withdrawal.

CESSATION OF SICKNESS BENEFITS AT AGES 65 AND 70

8. One of the early changes in benefit arrangements effected by many friendly societies after the passing of the National Insurance Act, 1911, was the adoption of tables for new entrants which provided for the cessation of sickness benefits at age 70. The need for action in this direction arose somewhat earlier than 1911 owing to the passing of the Old Age Pensions Act in 1908, but the provision of sickness benefits ceasing at age 70 under the State scheme served to focus the problem more clearly and rendered easier the passing of the necessary reforms. It will be readily understood that the receipt of a pension contemporaneously with a sickness benefit is likely to lead to an increase in the claims for the latter benefit, and it was the realization of this fact, and the recognition by those responsible for administering sickness benefits of the great difficulty of distinguishing between disability resulting merely from old age and that due to a specific ailment, that led most of the affiliated orders and of the other larger societies to adopt, in 1912 or thereabouts, tables for new entrants which provided for the cessation of sickness benefits at age 70, with or without an annuity benefit thereafter.

9. The passing of the Widows', Orphans' and Old Age Contributory Pensions Act, 1925, which provided for the grant of pensions at age 65 for a much larger section of the population than would have satisfied the means qualification of the original Act, has rendered the solution of the problem of excessive rates of sickness at the older ages still more urgent. It is obvious that as far as new members are concerned the proper course is to adopt new tables granting sickness benefits ceasing at age 65, but societies have been very hesitant to take this step. Many of them exhibit an unwillingness to invite new members to join on the basis of a sickness benefit ceasing at 65 which is not followed by an annuity, but they also maintain that the cost of the combined benefit is so heavy that it is not possible to secure new members upon such a basis. Even if societies were all to adopt for new entrants tables providing sickness benefits ceasing at age 65, they would still be left with the problem of the probable increase in claims after that age in respect of existing members assured for sickness benefits throughout life or up to the age of 70. Some few societies have substituted for sick pay after age 70 an annuity of equivalent value, but owing to the smallness of the annuity which can be allowed this solution has not proved to be popular. Where a society possesses a considerable surplus and the rate of reduced sick pay does not fall below one-half of full pay, it is sometimes practicable to apply the surplus in producing an annuity which the members are prepared to accept in commutation of sick pay, but it is unlikely that more than a small minority of societies can be persuaded to adopt this plan. The need to fix the commutation age at 65 instead of 70 reduces still further the attractiveness of the equivalent annuity.

10. There is an alternative method which it has been found possible to adopt in some few cases, viz. the grant of an endowment at age 65 or 70 in lieu of future sickness benefits. The amount of the endowment which can sometimes be granted is large enough to make this scheme popular, and it was recently adopted successfully in the case of a railway society where on retirement from service the members found it difficult to maintain their contributions. Indeed the same society recently adopted tables for new entrants granting sickness benefits to age 65 with an endowment at that age. So far the method of substituting an endowment at age 65 for future sickness benefits has however found little favour, and in some cases societies have been unwilling to adopt it on the ground that members who had exercised the option to commute their sickness benefits might be led to regret it by their subsequent experience of sickness.

It must be concluded that so far no really satisfactory scheme capable of general application has been devised for relieving societies of the heavy additional liability which appears likely to fall upon them in respect of members assured for sickness benefits beyond the age of 65.

CHANGES IN SICKNESS EXPERIENCE

11. A considerable amount of evidence is accumulating to show that the incidence of sickness claims over the different periods of life has altered to an important extent during the last 20 years. The evidence indicates that a heavy increase in sickness claims, as compared with the standard of the Manchester Unity Experience 1893–97, has taken place amongst the adult membership of friendly societies at the younger ages; this excess appears to decrease progressively as the period of middle life is approached. During this period light sickness claims are experienced, and this feature continues until old age is reached when a tendency to heavy claims is again liable to become apparent.

12. One of the most interesting problems which arises in connection with the question of the change in the incidence of sickness claims is the difference in the character of the sickness experiences which is often exhibited by members assured (*a*) under tables which have been recently adopted by societies, and (*b*) under tables previously in existence and now closed to new entrants. Investigation shows that there is a marked contrast between the experiences of the two sections of membership, the former group showing a much higher level of claims. Both groups, however, indicate a fairly rapid improvement in the experience as middle life is approached and in the case of the older membership, where the experience extends to the higher ages, the feature of heavy claims at the close of the table is noticeable.

BIBLIOGRAPHY

Sir George F. Hardy. "Essay on Friendly Societies." *J.I.A.* Vol. xxvii, p. 245.

Sir Alfred W. Watson. "The methods of analysing and presenting the Mortality, Sickness and Secession Experience of Friendly Societies." *J.I.A.* Vol. xxxv, p. 268.

—— *Account of an investigation of the Sickness and Mortality Experience of the I.O.O.F., Manchester Unity*, 1893–97. C. & E. Layton. Also *J.I.A.* Vol. xxxviii, pp. 369, 533.

—— "Some points of interest in the operations of Friendly Societies, Railway Benefit Societies and Collecting Societies." *J.I.A.* Vol xliv, p. 168.

—— "Analysis of a Sickness Experience." *J.I.A.* Vol. lxii, p. 12.

—— *Lectures on Friendly Society Finance*. C. & E. Layton.

W. P. Elderton and R. C. Fippard. *The Construction of Mortality and Sickness Tables*. A. & C. Black.

P. N. Harvey. "National Health Insurance Valuations." *J.I.A.* Vol. liv, p. 180. (Appendices A and B.)

Victor A. Burrows. "On Friendly Societies since the advent of National Health Insurance." *J.I.A.* Vol. lxiii, p. 307.

Vyvyan Marr. "Notes on an investigation of the Sickness and Mortality Experience of a Friendly Society." *T.F.A.* Vol. iv, p. 153.

Robert R. Brodie. "Some aspects of a fall in the rate of interest as affecting the liabilities of a Friendly Society." *T.F.A.* Vol. xii, p. 83.

—— "The effect of a change in the rate of mortality upon the value of sickness benefits." *J.I.A.* Vol. lxiv.

W. T. C. Blake. "The A B C of Friendly Society valuation." *J.S.S.* Vol. iv, p. 3.

"Friendly Societies"—the article in the 13th edition of the *Encyclopaedia Britannica*.